FOREWORD BY RYAN LEVESQUE
#1 NATIONAL BESTSELLING AUTHOR OF ASK

HOW TO DOUBLE YOUR CUSTOMERS, SALES & PROFITS WITH A/B TESTING

CONVERSION FANATIC

JUSTIN CHRISTIANSON
WITH MANISH PUNJABI

Conversion Fanatic

How To Double Your Customers, Sales and Profits With A/B Testing

Justin Christianson

with Manish Punjabi

Foreword: Ryan Levesque

#1 Bestselling Author of Ask

Copyright

For special discounts on bulk orders:
support@conversionfanatics.com

First Edition.
ISBN-13: 978-1517383183
ISBN-10: 1517383188

Editor: Michaela Zanello
Cover Art: Rob Secades, RobSecades@gmail.com

Connect With The Author

Facebook: Facebook.com/conversionfanatics

Twitter: @convfanatics

LinkedIn: conversionfanatics.com/linkedin

Email: support@conversionfanatics.com

Website: www.ConversionFanatics.com

Dedication

This book is dedicated to all the marketers and business owners out there that are constantly trying to provide the best product or service and will stop at nothing to be better daily.

Table Of Contents

Foreword

Ryan Levesque: #1 National Bestselling Author of Ask

Here's why you should be very excited about the book you're holding right now: it's your blueprint to immediately implementing successful split tests in your business—the kinds of tests that can double or even triple your response.

Over the years, I've had the pleasure of getting to know Justin Christianson and his partner, Manish Punjabi. They have decades of combined experience in digital marketing, running thousands of split tests for hundreds of different campaigns. In fact, I've referred several clients to them myself. Their relentless approach to testing has produced amazing results, and that's why I recommend them to my own 7, 8, and 9 figure clients.

When you think about a split test, it's essentially a type of feedback from your market. They're telling you, through numbers, which text, or offer, or design they prefer. And the idea of feedback is something that's very important to me, and something that I've devoted my business to perfecting.

My #1 National bestselling book, Ask, is based entirely on the concept of getting feedback from your market. The book teaches how to use quizzes and surveys to generate leads and sales online. Using this methodology, we generate over 52,000 email subscribers per day in 23 different markets.

Of course, we achieved those results not only by implementing the Ask Formula that I share in the book, but by a rigorous process of split testing and optimization.

I wish I'd had enough space in the book to emphasize just how important the process of split testing is to your business. I've invested the past 10 years of my life to optimizing this methodology, and over those past 10 years I've run a lot of split tests, including plenty of tests that have failed.

And yes, that's part of the process! Some people may argue that you learn just as much from the tests that fail as from the ones that succeed. But split tests that fail cost you time and money.

Wouldn't it be great if you could skip the tests that will fail, and go for the ones that have the best chance of success?

That's exactly what this book is for! And that's why you'll want to read it from cover to cover.

One of the fastest ways to succeed is by standing on the shoulders of giants, building on the work that others have done, so that you don't make the same mistakes.

And that's what Justin has provided in this book. He lays out his FULL testing methodology, as well as real-world valuable tests that you can implement in your marketing to shortcut your success.

In many ways this book is like a time machine, letting you skip weeks and months of wasted time and failed split tests, to jump ahead and know what works.

A/B testing is something most savvy marketers will tell you, "Yes, everyone should be split testing," but many of those marketers don't follow through consistently. And that's a shame, because for every day that goes by that you're not running a test, you're losing a valuable opportunity to grow your business.

In my experience, testing is something that should be built in to the fabric of your business. As a matter of fact, many of the core components of the Ask Formula were discovered through the process of split testing.

I tested, tweaked, and optimized my own process until I had what I now call the Ask Formula.

And guess what? I'm STILL optimizing, because I know the benefits of split testing:

- Many times, our best instincts will be totally WRONG. Testing lets the numbers decide what will work with your market.

- When you split test, you avoid wasting time and money on the things that are not converting.

- When you test, you're constantly improving your conversion rate and your results. Over time, this success builds to have a MAJOR effect on your business. And sometimes, you have a HUGE win that can double or even triple your results.

- Testing creates an atmosphere of creativity and innovation, where you and your team have the drive and motivation to try new ideas.

Now here's the good news: implementing and improving your testing process doesn't have to be difficult, and it doesn't have to be expensive and time-consuming.

This book is a practical how-to guide on split testing. Justin gives you the tools, methodology, and step-by-step checklist for running successful tests, including examples of what winning tests look like.

Follow the steps in this book and you will have everything you need to start running your first test. If you're already split testing, you'll have a much better idea of what to be testing next.

You have the opportunity, right now, to get your hands on real split test results from one of the leading experts in the field. If you care about your business, you should jump at this chance.

As a busy entrepreneur, I'm very discerning about the books I read and the people that I follow. I know you probably are too.

This book gets my highest recommendation.

Enjoy!

Ryan Levesque
#1 National Bestselling Author of Ask.

Introduction

"Never, never, never, never give up!"
~ Winston Churchill

In all things marketing, it all boils down to two simple things: traffic and conversions. In this book, we'll focus on the conversion side of that equation.

Which of these do you think converts better?

Version A - Control

Version B

Do you think you know the winning version?

One version is much simpler than the other. Version A has

several options to choose from while Version B only has one choice and that is to join the demo.

Version B actually converted 37.9% better than A! Tiny tweaks like this are holding down your customer count.

You may feel that giving your visitors options will give you a better chance but more options leads to friction. Friction leads to confusion and confusion lowers conversion rates and engagement.

As you can see from the results, it's not that the visitors didn't want it, they just had too many options. So they mostly likely left and looked at the competition.

But once the problem was fixed by making their decision simple, those digital "window-shoppers" converted into high quality leads.

Why was there such a huge difference in results?

The answer is because brand loyalty matters less for most online shoppers than ease of use, relevance, and persuasive design. The playing field continues to level.

Are you starting to see why conversion optimization matters to your online sales success? That's why I wrote this book, to help you realize the promise of higher conversion rates fast.

Conversion rate optimization is no longer an option if you still want to be in business in the next 1 to 5 years. If you're in a market of any reasonable size, where your potential customers are researching or buying online, then you're going to face stiff competition from marketers who are using these methods to grab your share of that pie.

When a prospective business approaches our agency for help, 9 times out of 10 what it thinks it has is a traffic problem. Traffic is everywhere, just get your credit card out and buy it.

What the business actually has is a conversion problem. It needs to get more visitors to take action—to read, to click, to call, to register, and of course to buy.

Getting more of your web visitors to take these desired actions is, after all, the name of the game. Without these desired actions, you don't have a business or a conversion funnel, you have fancy online brochure.

Now before you jump on my case about traffic not being the problem, let me clarify. Traffic can be the problem if you aren't targeting the right audience or you are buying junk traffic. When we say 'traffic' throughout the rest of this book, we're referring to targeted traffic—the right people who are actively looking for your product or service. We'll cover some key aspects of targeting your traffic in this book as well. After you have the groundwork of a proper conversion sequence in place, as having a proper path is perhaps the most over-looked aspect of conversions. We've helped companies reduce their traffic costs by as much as 90% with some simple targeting techniques.

The rest of this book is a culmination of over 20 years of combined online marketing experience between myself and my business partner, Manish Punjabi, who was a driving force behind getting this book written and contributed to many elements contained in it's pages. It's about the trial and error, the headaches, the sleepless nights, the success stories, and of course what we learned from working on hundreds of different marketing campaigns and thousands of different marketing tests.

Of course there were some failures too. Failures sometimes teach us more than the winners. Every failure, especially in optimization, is a chance to learn something, steer the ship, and ultimately come out on top.

We have a saying we like to quote about opportunity: "In every seed therein lies a forest of endless possibilities." It's our sincere hope that these ideas will be the seeds of greater fortune for you. We know they will help you increase your ROI and drive revenue for your company; we've seen it time and again.

This book is designed to give you a glimpse at what it takes to turn any idea into a profit-churning power house or take an existing business and help you realize the 2-10x leverage points that can help you grow. It's an in depth view of our process and what it takes to quickly experience tremendous growth in your sales. Some chapters are only a few pages while others are many more. I hope you enjoy the following pages and the ideas help you realize the importance of true conversion rate optimization.

Onwards.

Justin Christianson

ONE
Predictable, Repeatable Growth

_____

"I've found that luck is quite predictable. If you want more luck, take more chances. Be more active. Show up more often."
~ Brian Tracy

The goal of your site should be to get people to take a desired action, whether that is to fill out a form to get more information, request a demo, opt-in with their email address in exchange for something of value, or the ultimate catalyst, to get their credit card out to give you money.

If you can get your site to meet your goals, whatever they may be, then your next thought is going to be to pour rocket fuel on the fire by getting more people to the site as fast as humanly possible. But you need to do so in a way that is predictable and scalable, otherwise you're going to go broke. The question is, is it possible?

We like to think so, but in order to do so you need to do a few things first. The first thing is to find out exactly what your potential customers want. What makes them tick? What keeps them up at night?

Then, give them the solution to their most pressing needs or desires.

Cash-flow and Profits Come From Learning:

One of our philosophies is that learning is power, and often, we say that learning what doesn't work in your marketing campaigns is better than learning what does work.

Did you know that 95% of websites out there track user data in some fashion, yet less than 30% actually do something with the data they collect? That's sad if you ask me.

The biggest catalyst in a profitable marketing campaign is your users. Your users will tell you what they want to see and what they don't want to you; you just have to know what to look for and then use that data in your favor.

It could be as easy as sending them a survey to ask them a few questions, or you may have to look at other information, such as bounce rate, user flow, click data, scrolling reports, time spent on page, percentage watched on a video, and many others.

Sometimes, it isn't black and white, but if you are collecting information, the answers are typically there.

You don't know what you don't know, and that is the problem, but that is also the beauty of leveraging the Internet; you can quickly find what you are looking for—the problem areas and holes in your leaky bucket—and fix them.

When it comes to increasing your cash-flow for your business, it comes down to learning more about your visitors, prospects, and customers.

By getting to know more about your potential customers, the better it is that you can present what you have to offer as the solution to what they are looking for.

It could be that you sell software, weight loss, cell phone accessories, security solutions, nutraceuticals, or even services.

What you sell doesn't matter as much (even though your product needs to be good) as it matters how well you communicate that to your audience.

The only downfall is that it often takes time to gather enough data to find out what works best.

This is why so many campaigns fail in the beginning; they don't gather enough information to make educated changes to appeal to a larger audience.

Driving a few clicks from a PPC campaign to a landing page and not getting results doesn't mean you have failed. It just means you don't have enough data to show them what it is they really want.

From the ad creative to the landing page messaging, all the way through to product delivery, each step is an opportunity to learn. And like I said, learning is power.

Once you have data, you can then make changes to your campaign and offer to appeal to a larger audience.

Is price a bigger factor than you thought? Do visitors like video or text better? Are they actually seeing my offer in the video?

Find the bottlenecks by looking at your information collected and don't be like the 70+% of people who don't do anything with it.

Give your campaigns enough time, tweak it accordingly, and watch your cash-flow increase.

At the end of the day, no matter what you are selling, you are dealing with people.

People just like you and I—people with problems who are in search of a solution. The minute you start thinking about things that way, instead of just numbers on a spreadsheet, you are ahead of the vast majority of marketers.

By identifying what your customers want it makes it much easier to get them to take a desired action, such as, again, giving you money.

It is proven that people buy for two reasons: to avoid a pain or to gain pleasure. That's it!

To avoid a pain or to gain pleasure—think about that for a second. Now think about how that applies to your business and what you are offering.

Are you helping your potential customers solve a pain or gain pleasure?

If you can figure out what the pain or pleasure is and deliver the solution your customers are looking for in the form of your product or service, you will win the game of marketing.

It doesn't matter whether you are selling software or

supplements that help with joint pain as long as you are connected to the minds of your prospects.

Getting in the minds of your prospective customers allows you to predictably sell more of what it is that you have to sell. Then you can sell your customers other complimentary products, and then basically repeat the process time and time again.

The bigger the pain or pleasure, the easier it is to sell a solution.

But the question is, how do you do it?

It makes no difference what you think. All that matters is what your prospects think, what they want, and what they will pay to get it.

There are a few ways to figure out exactly what your prospects want, which we will cover in more detail throughout the following pages.

One of the biggest ways is to simply ask them. If you already have a product or service that is selling, simply asking your existing customers what they prefer will help you cater your messaging to be more effective with a larger audience of prospects.

Your existing customers are the biggest catalyst when it comes to whether you will succeed or fail. They have already taken the plunge and given you money. They have experienced what you have to offer, how you work, the processes, and the end result.

Now some business owners simply don't want to know what their customers have to say because they are afraid of the negative consequences, the bad feedback they might get, or worst case, a customer wants a refund.

There is a big difference between getting a negative review and private feedback from an existing customer.

Most customers will be happy to give you feedback in a private setting, and in some cases, it will provide them with an outlet to vent some frustrations about doing business with you and stifle them from making their frustrations public.

Remember earlier when we talked about failures sometimes being better than winners?

The same applies here with getting feedback from customers. The negative feedback helps you put a finger on the pulse of your business, uncover hidden problem areas, and it gives you a roadmap of where you can be better.

Overall it is a win/win no matter how painful it might be to get some of the feedback.

You can deploy this strategy in several ways: the most common being in the form of a survey. Simply send out a survey via email asking for help from your customers. Everyone wants to help, or at least they should.

Pro Tip: Offer something of value in exchange for feedback to get more responses.

TWO

Becoming A World Class Company

"World-Class performers have no plan B. Failure just isn't an option." ~ Robin Sharma

In creating a world-class offer or company and multiplying your sales and dominating your market without overly increasing your stress and workload, you need to think and behave like a world-class company.

Leverage your efforts so you can move up the entrepreneurial ladder and turn your business into the thriving enterprise so you can make more and work less.

So how do you do it? Well, you need to understand the pillars, which we will cover in this chapter in more detail.

But first, in a perfect world, when looking at a market you may think that the "share" of the market is pretty much uniform fashion. As illustrated in the below figure, the leader in the market has the most sales, and each company respectively has its own share.

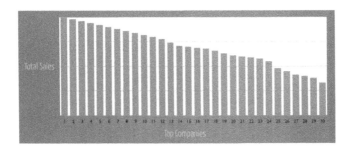

This of course isn't the case in the real world. There is no "gap" at all. Oh, how amazing it would be if it were like that.

But instead, as you can see in the following figure, there is a BIG "gap" where the top 3-5 companies control most of the market, basically leaving the scraps for the rest of the companies.

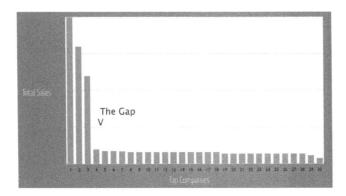

Now don't get me wrong, there are plenty of companies that are happy with the "scraps" left over, and depending on the market you are in, those scraps could be enough to sustain and grow a multi-million-dollar-per-year business.

But who really wants to be left with scraps? We want to control the market, be a market leader, and reap the rewards that being a market leader offers.

Top-tier, world-class companies always win. They take the lion's share of the market, and having a top-tier company allows you to be less busy working in your business and leaves you free to lead, plan for the future, and focus on furthering your growth.

Having the elements of a top-tier, world-class company gives you more control of your business—you know your numbers—and because of that the financial results become more predictable.

All top-tier, world-class companies have the following pillars:

A Viable Product:

Ok, so this shouldn't be a big surprise for you, but it needs to be said, because without it, all the other strategies are supporting something that's empty at its core and the business will ultimately fail.

Even if the sales numbers aren't stellar - you need to start with SOMETHING, and a good product is the foundation of everything that comes after.

We're not going to dwell on this but I do want to say.

You don't have to have a MILLION DOLLAR IDEA. You

just need a solid product (or service) that fulfills the following criteria:

It's in a proven niche:

If something is "too new", that's not usually a good thing. People trying to come up with "Million Dollar Ideas" are usually trying to come up with something SO new that they consciously steer away from things that people are actually already buying.

A good rule of thumb is to build a business around something people are ALREADY buying.

Remember:

Google wasn't the first search engine, Facebook wasn't the first social network, and Amazon wasn't the first online bookseller.

You DON'T need to invent a new market. It's far easier, and far more profitable to tap into a market that's already there.

It's something people actually want.

This ties into what I just mentioned, but there's a subtle difference.

I can't tell you how many struggling entrepreneurs I meet who are out there trying to sell something nobody wants.

They may have a product that people actually NEED. It might be useful and helpful.

It has a unique twist or hook

Ok, so where's the room for originality?

It's here.

You DO need to differentiate, but the best way to differentiate is not by coming up with a solution to a problem nobody knows about.

It's by having a 'better' or 'different' solution than what else is out there.

Believe it or not, it's possible to build massive businesses WITHOUT this, but it's harder and it's a lot less fun to launch a copycat product or service.

It Actually Delivers

If not just for your own sense of integrity and your own passion in growing your business, you need to know that your product WORKS.

And many businesses have done quite well without this one, but ultimately for a sustainable business, your product must deliver some benefit to your customers.

Scalable Systems:

If your sales increased 10X tomorrow could you handle the growth?

You need to position your company for growth no matter how big or how small you are now. Being able to handle an increase in growth is what will set you as a world-class company. Plus being positioned for growth will better help with the growth from optimizing your sales campaigns.

Scalable systems are basically recurring problems that need to be handled again and again and again.

You must have systems in place, whether they are technology systems or people systems. Having these elements in place, having things to handle the recurring elements is what will allow you to free up time to focus on growth.

The right systems free up your time while improving quality control in every aspect of your business.

They automate the processes in your business and remove "you" from the equation so you're free to focus on other things (whether that means golfing more or growing the business).

Typically, businesses plateau because the owners or the people running the show are spread so thin that they don't have the time, the energy, or the mental space to think about what's next for the business.

So when I go into work with a new client, my first goal is to create the systems for them that will free up their time. A big selling point of our services is that we alleviate bandwidth issues that cause companies to not be testing and optimizing enough.

If you're making $15K a month and working 60 hours a week and you can get to where you're still making $15K a month but only have to work 10 hours a week for it, THAT'S when you're poised for the next phase of growth and can move on to the next strategy.

So if systems are SO CRUCIAL to building a top-tier business, why is it that so many businesses aren't using systems as much as they should be using them?

They don't know that they need them—most people are focused only on sales and they ignore systems; hence as they get more customers, the problems only grow, and the business inevitably bottlenecks and collapses.

You can't use this excuse anymore.
And yes, optimization is a system!

1. They're focused on putting out fires rather than setting things up for growth

(Even though the business owner will save you lots of time down the road, it takes less time in the moment to DO something than it does to write out a procedure for it, so a lot of business owners get stuck putting out fires. You need to make time to set up systems or you'll forever be trying to hold everything together by yourself.)

2. They don't know where to start or what to do

(This is a big one. they're not sure which systems they need and how to create one so they put it off and put it off and years go by while they waste thousands of hours doing the same tasks they could've easily had someone do for them with the right system)

3. They think they have to do it all themselves

The good news is that you can have your TEAM create most of the systems for your business as they do their jobs.

And that's one of the things we help businesses with. We give some simple instructions to their workers so the workers create the systems as they go. It's actually better to do it this way because the workers are the ones who'll be using the systems anyway.

I can't stress enough the importance of having the right systems in place before you move on to the next strategy.

The relief you feel at knowing your business is a well-oiled machine that can handle anything that comes its way is unbelievable. It creates a feeling of having a "real business" rather than just a website that makes some money.

Plus, it gives you the peace of mind that if for some reason you couldn't work, whether it's because you had to go on a trip or got sick or whatever, you'd continue to make money from your business.

And this freedom allows you to focus on GROWTH.

BUT remember, this is just the foundation on which you're going to build your skyscraper. With these systems in place, you're ready to move on to the real secret to hitting the tipping point of exponential growth.

Optimization:

First off, 'conversion rate' means the percentage of visitors who take a desired action on your website, which could be any of the following:

Clicking on an Ad

Opting-in with their email address

Hitting The "Add To Cart" Button

Entering their credit card info and Making a Purchase

Adding an upsell to their purchase

It's whatever action you want them to take that you believe will lead to the desired key performance indicator.

You can probably see how split-testing could be valuable, after all, this book is all about it, but let me just drive home why it's so important that you're using split-testing for your online sales funnels.

It's the only way to know for SURE what will improve conversions.

It's amazing when you actually start testing. You realize how WRONG your instincts are about what's going to improve your marketing.

No matter how much you "think" you know, you can always be proven wrong, as I am time and time again. It still amazes me just what will have an overall impact on conversions—things like button color changes, headline changes, removing form fields, layout changes, and images. Nothing in optimization is off limits.

Split-testing takes the guesswork out of boosting your sales; you know for sure what works because you've tested it.

Secondly, because you know for sure, you can continue to test different variations and continue to improve your conversion rates to get bigger and bigger boosts to your sales.

It's important to keep growing because if YOU'RE not and your competition is, you can get crowded out of the market very quickly.

Split-testing allow you to get and keep a competitive advantage, which is something you need in an ever-changing, fast-paced digital marketing world.

THREE

You Don't Have A Traffic Problem

"Traffic is the oxygen. Yes, you need it, but traffic (like oxygen) is not exactly a rare commodity." ~ *Ken McCarthy*

As mentioned in the introduction, when the majority of our clients approach us for help it isn't because they have a traffic problem; they have a conversion problem.

Traffic is actually pretty easy at least for the most part. There is a TON of it out there, just buy it. Pretty much every major site out there, including Google, Facebook, Instagram, Reddit, Plenty Of Fish, Outbrain, even Forbes and other major sites, have traffic programs.

You simply have to do your research and find out where your target audience is hanging out and push your message out in front of them on these available platforms.

In order to predictably grow, you need to get a handle on your conversions and strive to increase those conversions.

But conversions start with traffic—the right traffic and optimizing that traffic for a better message, higher click-through rate, and getting the right people to see our offer.

We have a saying and that is "If you aren't converting at 100%, then you aren't done optimizing." We have yet to see that happen, so therefore we continue to try—more leads, more sales, and then getting your customers to buy more stuff. After all, isn't that the name of the game?

In order to do this you need to optimize the traffic you are getting through split-testing or conversion rate optimization.

Conversion optimization, just in case you don't know, is the method of creating an experience for a website or landing page visitor with the goal of increasing the percentage of visitors that **convert** into leads and/or customers.

Or, in simpler terms, conversion optimization is getting web visitors to do more of what you want, providing a clear path to the end goal or desired action you are looking to achieve from your visitors.

When I say most people have a conversion problem, that basically means they can't get enough people to give them money, and as a result, they are spending too much money on advertising and will eventually go broke trying. So you have to push yourself toward the "tipping point," which we will cover here in a little bit.

There are a couple things you need to know about conversion

rate optimization, and probably the biggest reason most people fail at doing it.

First is time. It is our only limiting factor. You need to not only have enough traffic but you also need to have enough time and patience to see a test through to becoming statistically significant.

Giving your marketing enough time and effort:

In marketing, especially when you are dealing with paid media, time is your only real limiting factor.

Wouldn't it be great if you launched a new campaign and immediately all the numbers somehow magically worked out in your favor, meaning you automatically put in $1 and made $2, $3, $4? Sure, it happens on occasion but it's rare. If it were like that all the time, then we wouldn't be in business, and there would be far more super successful companies out there.

Instead, what happens is you launch your campaign and find yourself spending $50 to acquire a customer while you make back only $40, essentially losing $10 for every new customer.

What we find is most people would give that up and mark it off as a failure. But smart marketers know that they are very close to a winner and keep pushing, tweaking, testing, and dialing in the campaign.

Tweak your targeting, test the messaging, tweak your upsell path, and before you know it, you'll be spending $20 and returning $100.

Of course these are just example numbers, and each business is different.

Aside from being able to hang on long enough financially, the only problem here is time.

Things don't happen overnight. Remember, most businesses deal with the same common denominator, which is people.

It takes time to allow enough people to see your ads, to click-through to your landing page, and to ultimately take action.

Often, companies come to us thinking we have the 'magic' button that will somehow put their campaign into serious profit mode, but they want it done in days instead of the weeks or even months that it sometimes takes.

If you have a viable product, almost every campaign can be dialed in to be profitable but only if you give it enough time.

Typically, there are many elements to a successful campaign that all have to be working together for maximum efficiency and profit.

Even if you have a campaign working, there are always ways to improve the results of that campaign through testing.

The example we give is a company that came on to have us improve its already successful results. The company said, "If you could increase our output 25%, you would be our best friend." The company is already successful, but it knows that through strategic testing, it can be better and more profitable, and looking at its sales process, we have already discovered several areas that will increase engagement and ultimately sales all the while increasing the efficiency of the company's ad spend.

When talking about time, it is the same for a split-testing plan.

Often, we are anxious about getting to the end result instead of giving the test enough time to work through its course, and not allowing for this could actually have a negative result.

Example: You setup an A/B test that is testing some images on a landing page.

A. Control

B. New Image

After about 1,000 clicks you see a handful of conversions and the new image quickly jumps out into the lead, winning by 25%.

Some people would say, "Great we got a winner," immediately making the new image the new control.

There is, however, ONE BIG problem. Yep, you guessed it: TIME!

They didn't allow the test to run out to be statistically significant. They only had a few conversions on each variation, which simply isn't enough data. Typically, you need to look for 25 conversions on each variation before you even start looking further.

Here is an example of when this happened:

While running a client campaign we were testing a video on the checkout page basically telling people what to do, how to contact support, etc.

On day 1, the new video was showing an increase of more than 33%. But can you guess what happened?

By the end of day 2 that video started to slip and began losing by more than 20%.

If we would have turned off the test and determined the video to be a winner, we would have potentially lost more than 20% of our conversions, thinking we were improving things by more than 33%.

See what I mean? Time!

You have to give your marketing campaigns enough time to truly see the results you are looking for.

Second is focus. Often, people focus on just one element of their sales process and don't follow that up with tests to the rest of the funnel. The result could be higher conversion rates on the front, but that could actually lead to you making less money at the end.

For example, if you have a lead generation campaign running tied to a product that you are selling for $40, then you decide to remove some form fields on your opt-in form, and as a result, you boost your lead generation conversion rate 50%. But then, you fail to pay attention to the conversion rate on your $40 product. Sure, you are getting more leads, but your sales conversion dropped by 20%.

Same thing goes for upsells. You have the same $40 product, and in an effort to increase your sales, you cut the price down to $30. Sales go up 15%, but as a result, half of the people are saying yes to your upsell, again leaving you with less revenue.

It is important that you look at the entire sales process and optimize everything consecutively, paying attention to what matters most, which is revenue per customer and your earnings per click.

Third is bandwidth. You know you should test; it's important.

But you get busy on other projects and neglect what matters most, which is getting more out of your digital marketing efforts.

You would be absolutely shocked at the amount of people spending serious money on advertising and their absolute disregard for their optimization—companies spending millions of dollars each month without a single split-test. It makes me sick to think about it, but sadly many are basically flying blind but still manage to make it work.

Imagine you are a company that is generating leads in the financial market. You are spending $1 million dollars per month on ads with an average click cost of $5, and on average, you are getting a 1% conversion rate on your landing pages, meaning you get 200,000 clicks and 2,000 leads from that. Keep in mind this is just an example, a real world example mind you.

What would it look like for your business if you were getting even a 20% increase in the number of leads generated?

200,000 clicks at a 1.2% conversion rate brings you 2,400 leads instead of 2,000 on the same ad spend.

Not paying attention to your conversion rate and more importantly how to increase that conversion rate could mean, in this example, millions of dollars in additional return on the advertising investment.

Bottom line is that it is vitally important to constantly be striving for better daily.

The fourth is not using their given data. It is said that 97% of websites collect data in some way, shape, or form but less than 30%

actually use the information to improve their results.

Pay attention to your numbers, look at them, follow them, and find out where people are coming from, where they are going, and where they are dropping off.

I will mention this several times in the pages of this book, but you can't assume anything—let your visitors guide you with their actions and couple that with some best practices and hypothesis and you will have a winning formula for better results.

In conversion optimization, anything goes and even the smallest thing can make the biggest difference. We are talking about layout of the page, text, headline, images, proof elements, colors, styles, sizes, menus, footer, video, no video, steps in the form, price, guarantee, offer, bonuses, and the list goes on and on.

When I say even the smallest change can make a difference, I go back to the story of a company selling music lessons, long before the days of the Internet.

For months they ran the ad "Put Music In Your Life." One day the person in charge of placing the newspaper ad misspelled the headline

Instead it read "Puts Music In Your Life." The result of this little blunder? How about triple the amount of sales.

If one little "S" in a headline can make that much of a difference, what can changes to your site do?

The reason they figured was because the main headline conveyed some "work" involved, while the second, winning headline conveyed the work being done for them. BIG difference.

Easy outsells hard every day of the week. So the more you can relate the simplicity of your solution, even if it's subconsciously, the better off you will be.

There is a reason the "magic pills, potions, and lotions" in the weight loss industry constantly tout words like "easy," "simple," "fast," "shortcuts," et cetera.

Is weight loss typically easy? No, it takes dedication. But the vast majority of "buyers" in that market are looking for a simple solution. So what do you do? Give them what they are looking for.

Now you have the other side of the coin with products like P90X where they tell you flat out it is the hardest thing you are going to do, but if you do it, you will get the results you are looking for.

But most people don't know that they failed 400+ times before finding a winning offer, which has gone on to sell MILLIONS!

Yep, they optimized and they won!

So how do you get more? Well, you have to split-test and split-test fast and hard. After all, time is money.

Analyze your data, find those pain or pleasure points, throw in a little simplicity, and TEST! Nothing is off limits. Figure out what makes your visitors tick, what they respond to more, and continually try to beat your previous high score.

Now there are plenty of tools to help you with this and there definitely is a science to it.

Since we have been doing this for years, we have a baseline test swipe file of what we have found to move the conversion needle the most, and believe it or not, it works across the majority of industries we have tried it in.

As we get more in depth, we will share how to create infinite tests and reveal some of our best practices.

But before we continue, repeat this to yourself: "I will split-test everything I can, and I won't stop until I reach 100%."

You would be amazed at just how many people don't pay that close attention to their conversion rates and optimizing them. I am talking even the biggest companies spending millions per month on advertising.

Don't think that it is "good enough." Imagine a 10, 20, or 30%+ lift in your sales day after day, month after month. It makes a big difference, doesn't it? And in most cases, this increase is straight to the bottom line.

As an example, we had a client generating about 600 leads per day. Out of that about 4% were buying the client's product.

We tested one little thing: highlighting the submit button on the landing page. The result was a 30% boost in leads, leading to over $1,900 per day in revenue—no more traffic but plenty more revenue.

One simple change!

See the importance?

In order to split-test, it is important that you understand the basics of your metrics or in this case…

FOUR

Know Thy Numbers

"In God we trust. All others bring data."

~ W.E. Deming

I can't even count the number of times clients have come to us needing help with their conversions, and after digging a little, we've come to find out they have no clue what their numbers are.

And some of these clients have massive advertising budgets but they still don't know their metrics.

Of course we like these types of clients, as we can usually come in, find some places they are bleeding, and come out looking like heroes because we cut their acquisition costs in half and dramatically improved their businesses.

We have even been asked, "What can I expect for ROI from optimizing?"

Well, it really depends but it is much easier to find out if you know your numbers.

Example: Say you are spending on average, in the case of a former client, $80 to acquire a new customer. Out of every 2,000 people, 40 people become a customer, meaning you have a 2% conversion rate.

You know that the average customer is worth $160 at 6 months.

It will take you on average 3 months from the time a new customer comes in the door to break even on your ad spend.

Most companies can't wait that long, and if you didn't have a good handle on your metrics, you would never know this crucial information. In some cases you might call this campaign a failure.

Now let's look at what optimizing looks like from a numbers standpoint to see if it actually was a failure.

We switched up the targeting, and tested new offers and landing page elements, and the result was pretty staggering.

Instead of paying $80 to acquire a new customer (CPA: Cost per acquisition), we cut it down to about $10 on average. So instead of 3 months to break-even, the client was profitable from almost day one.

We took it a step further through on-site testing and brought the conversion rate up from 2% to over 3.5%, or about a 75% lift.

Out of the same 2,000 visitors, instead of 40 new customers, the client getting close to 70 new customers.

We were then able to scale the campaigns up to close to 400, and at the peak, 700 daily sales, which were much more profitable.

But all of that wouldn't have been possible if we didn't know the numbers of the campaign.

Starting to see how important this is now?

The true winners in any market know their metrics down to the finest detail and they aren't just numbers on a spreadsheet either.

Knowing your metrics uncovers great areas in need of improvement. Knowing your numbers can show you things like what advertising methods are working, what isn't working, how much you can spend to acquire a customer, what a lead is worth to you, when a customer is profitable in the lifecycle, friction points in the checkout process, and the list goes on and on.

The more you have a handle on, the better you are going to be.

Have you ever heard the saying, "He or she who markets best wins?"

Well, in order to market best you need to know your numbers.

A former client of mine, who runs a wildly successful online training company in a sports-related niche, once told me after we discontinued working together that "We are going to just out convert them, so we can buy all the traffic in the market."

What he meant by this was that he was going to get his conversion rate up so high that he could basically spend more to acquire a customer, virtually buying up all the available traffic and leaving scraps for the competition.

So far, he has done a great job of doing it. When you know your numbers you can afford to spend more because you know what a lead and customer is worth to you on day 1, in 1 month, in 3 months, in 6 months, in 1 year, and over a lifetime.

We run across campaigns all the time where a company is not profitable on day 1 of acquiring a customer, but they know their numbers enough that they can go upside down to get that customer on day 1 and make up for it in future purchases.

It's sort of like the law of averages.

This is where we find most companies fall short, especially when launching a new advertising campaign. For the sake of example they spend $1,000 on a new campaign and only make back $600 in initial revenue. They immediately think this campaign is a loser.

Smart marketers know their numbers and can see the campaign has serious potential.

Say the initial customer value was $100. So in this example 6 new customers were acquired for the $1,000 spent.

In other words, the acquisition cost was just over $166. One-hundred and sixty-six dollars was spent to make $100 on day 1 customer value and this was chalked up to a failed campaign. After all, you can't spend more than you are making.

Lucky for you, you are one of those smart marketers and know your numbers. You understand that the 6-month customer value is over $300 based on average additional purchases.

So instead of a failed campaign, you know that you will be profitable on that same customer within 6 months, actually quite profitable.

Through some tweaking, you can then bring down the $166 a bit more and be profitable a bit quicker and have a true winning campaign on your hands.

All this is possible because, again, you know your numbers.

The name of the game is to bring your acquisition cost down and your average value up.

A good example of this is in the lead generation game. A client of ours was selling a huge software system to alleviate IT downtime for corporations.

The client was willing to spend up to $250 per lead. We are not talking about customers here. We are talking about a lead.

The client had his numbers dialed in enough to know that each lead was worth more to him than $250, so were willing to spend that much to get one.

Again, it is all possible because of knowing the numbers.

Here are some key numbers to make sure you know:

Lead and customer acquisition costs, initial customer value, 30, 60, 90, 1-year, lifetime customer value, per lead value

In most cases, you want to try and get the initial customer value to be greater than the cost per acquisition, meaning the money you collect from the initial purchase plus any upsells or cross sells is greater than what it costs you to acquire that customer or the ad spend.

This will help you endlessly acquire more customers because you are basically paying for your advertising.

Where you make your money is on the back-end, either

through recurring subscriptions, selling more products such as premium upgrades or complimentary additions, or even up selling your customers into larger ticket items such as coaching.

Where some people fall short is they are afraid to spend money to acquire customers and consequently lose money, meaning they spend $20 to acquire a customer who only spends $15 resulting in a $5 loss per customer.

I know those are small numbers, but in order to make things work, you need to look at the entire picture.

How can you increase that customer value from $15 to something more like $30?

In order to do this, again, you need to try several things: increase your price, add upsells, and/or sell more products in the follow-up to bring that 1 month and beyond value up.

Another good example of this is a software client of ours, who sells a software as a service, which starts with a free trial.

This client knows that a customer is worth roughly $335 over the course of the first 6 months on average.

So the client is willing to spend more to acquire a free trial customer and possibly lose money on each new customer for the first couple months.

This opens things up to allow our client to spend more money on ads and still be profitable—not on day 1 or even the first 2 months but in the long-run.. Of course it wouldn't be possible if the client didn't know his numbers.

Now, if you only have one product, it is going to be difficult to pay for traffic and actually be profitable unless of course your product is on a recurring model, as in our SaaS example.

Pay attention to your numbers. As Warren Buffet says, "You need to speak the language of money."

Knowing even the basic metrics can steer you in the right direction for a successful online campaign as opposed to chalking it up as a failure.

FIVE

Tipping Point

"The name given to that one dramatic moment when everything can change all at once is the tipping point." ~Malcolm Gladwell

Once you know the key metrics, you can look to reach the tipping point. Basically, the tipping point means that your earnings per click exceed your cost per click.

Or, in other words, if you earn more than what it costs you, you have positive ROI.

By reaching the tipping point you can do the following:

Afford more traffic

Get faster and more dramatic split-test results

Afford to outbid your competition

Attract more and better affiliates

Afford to invest more in growth

Add more back-end products

Build new funnels

Enter new markets

All of this wouldn't be possible unless you know your numbers. As W. Clement Stone said, "In god we trust, all others must bring data."

Knowing your numbers is crucial to a successful campaign; without knowing them you are basically flying blind.

Commitment to breaking through, why bother to learn from direct response

"You're either growing or dying,
there ain't no third direction"
~Tommy Boy

If you are going to start a campaign or even work to improve an existing one, you need to have patience and a strong commitment to breaking through to the other side.

It isn't very often that you come out of the gate, have a true winner, and hit a home run. No matter how good you are.

It takes time to dial in a campaign. As I tell people, time is our only limiting factor. Start with your best effort, spend a little on traffic, test and tweak, and you will have a winner soon enough.

I am firm believer in the thought of, you don't have to get it right, you just have to get it going.

Getting something out into the marketplace regardless of how "pretty" is better than trying to make it perfect. Like I said, give it your best shot—your best chance at a winner—gather data, and tweak things until you get it dialed in.

Take a page out of the playbook of direct response marketers. In direct response, it is often highly competitive, traffic can often be expensive, but the true winners win BIG!

When I say direct response, I am not talking about e-commerce online retail stores. I am referring to the info marketers of the world or even the highly successful supplement companies. Those who are driving traffic to a single product offering as opposed to those who are sending people to an online store with multiple product options.

Why bother to learn the ins and outs of direct response marketing?

Well frankly, the top direct response marketers know their numbers, they know what makes their target market tick, and they know how to sell.

They know how to put together good offers that gets results.

As we briefly touched on in the introduction, it absolutely does not matter what you are offering in your business as a product or service.

We say that with this in mind: your product has to deliver what it promises, and even better, it has to over deliver. You know the saying, "under promise, over deliver."

You can't throw junk into the marketplace and expect to grow a sustainable business around it.

What I mean by that statement is simple. If you charge $100, you better deliver 10 times that in value.

That is the first step in the process—a good solid product you stand behind and would be happy if your mother bought it.

So what exactly makes a good offer? To get to that we must first look at why people do what they do. What makes a person make a fabled buying decision and part with their hard earned money?

It's human nature for people to make buying decisions based on two reasons.

The first is to gain pleasure. Buying that product or services gives them a sense of pleasure. For example a person may buy a brand new sports car, a quality chocolate bar, or maybe even a vacation.

Taking ownership or consuming such products gives the buyer a sense of pleasure. It gives them that warm and fuzzy feeling and a sense of accomplishment in their purchase.

The second is to avoid pain. This is actually the bigger reason why people buy, but it is important to understand both.

A person may buy a product to avoid pain… They have a headache so they buy a bottle of aspirin, they purchase training on how to make money online because they are tired of their financial situation.

Or we can bring back the car example. A person may buy a new car because they are tired of taking the bus or maybe their car doesn't always start and they need to get to work.

The higher the level of pain and the better your product or service can solve that problem the better off you are going to be.

To begin to formulate a good offer you must first identify what exactly those pain or pleasure points are that your product or service can provide, as discussed earlier.

Do you solve a pain point or do you provide pleasure? If so what?

Once you have established exactly where your product or service fits it is then your job to market that product effectively and convey the proper messaging and price to get the prospective buyer to take the desired action you are looking for, which at the end of the day is to give you money.

When looking to create a good offer, there are many different aspects you need to look at in as far as the sales message goes.

When I look at a marketing campaign, I tend to look immediately at what is being offered and how it is being offered to get a sense of where to begin optimizing—working backwards from there.

How is your offer being presented?

Is there a clear and concise value proposition, meaning are you presenting your offer in a way that the perceived value is felt to be much higher than the price tag?

In the head of your prospective buyer, is it a good value for the money spent?

If you do your job correctly in presenting the value proposition versus the actual price tag, you are usually in good shape.

In most cases, if you do this step right, price is not a factor.

Often, the case is that we can raise the price by 50-100% and actually keep a similar conversation rate, which is due to the fact that the product and offer does a good job at solving the problem, and the value is perceived to be much greater.

Chances are that in your market there are going to be some competitors. Well, there better be because that usually means there is money being spent.

Another way to make sure your value and offer are there is to set a differentiator. In other words, how does your product differ from others in the market? What makes your product better?

AG Lafley, the CEO of Proctor and Gamble, said in his book *Playing To Win* that there are only two ways to win. The first is the beat them on price, which means you are the cheapest on the market. And the second, which is what we are talking about here, is to have a differentiator.

At our agency, we aren't exactly the cheapest, but we make up for it in customer service, attention to detail, and results.

If you don't already have something that sets yourself apart from the rest and are trying to be competitive on price, you are in for an uphill battle.

Think about your offer and how you can set yourself apart. I have mentioned a few ways here.

A good example of setting yourself apart comes from a former client in a highly competitive sports training niche. The content and training is great, and people love his stuff and buy from him over and over again.

There are other products in the market that teach what it is that he teaches, but he sets himself apart through his guarantee.

The competition are all offering 30, 60, 90=day guarantees. He took it a step further and guarantees his products and results for life.

He is the only one with enough courage to throw that guarantee out there, and as a result, he is a market leader.

What else is selling in your market that is similar? Find out what your competitors are doing and highlight why yours is different and better.

Think about your differentiators and make sure those elements come across in your offer as one of the big selling points.

SIX

Conversion Funnel Breakdown

"The job of the conversion funnel is to progress visitors through it at maximum speed and with minimum effort." *~Unkown*

Sales funnels can come in all shapes and sizes, from the most basic lead generation funnel all the way to funnels with hundreds of steps and intricate details and paths.

Luckily, we live in a day and age when technology can be setup in a way to do the majority of the heavy lifting.

For example, in the early to mid-2000s, providing one-click upsells was difficult and often a manual process, if you even knew about the concept, to do one-click upsells.

Today, the majority of the out-of-the-box shopping carts and CRM's come with the capabilities built right in.

We are fortunate to be close friends with one of the pioneers of the one-click upsell process (at least in the direct response world), Matt Gill. Back when he first started doing one-click upsells, he had it setup in a way that looked like a one-click upsell, but in reality, he was manually entering the credit card information again on the back-end to process another payment for the upgraded product. It was a painful manual process to say the least.

But the process worked, and as a result, it started the trend of pretty much became commonplace in many markets, with many shopping carts, plugins, and other tools making it super simple.

This one-click process was responsible for an almost 500% growth in revenue for my former company.

Companies like Apple with iTunes and Amazon make the one-click buy even easier.

Luckily, again, we have the ability to automate the process now easier than ever.

The purpose of a sales funnel is as the name suggests. It is designed to pour people (visitors) into the top of the funnel and push them down a path of taking a desired action (i.e. becoming a lead and/or buying from you).

As previously mentioned, sales funnels come in all shapes and sizes but are a vital element to increasing your sales results. Let's look at a sales funnel in its simplest form, starting with a lead magnet or ethical bribe.

Think of a sales funnel as GPS for your business.

You hop in the car, punch in your destination, and the lovely voice guides you step-by-step to your desired destination.

A sales funnel should do the same thing and it starts with your ads.

Going back to solving problems, your ad should highlight the solution to these problems, or the final destination.

Once a person clicks on the ad, he or she is taken to step 1 (the top of the funnel) — a landing page that further highlights the pain points and the benefits/solutions you have for his or her problem.

The more congruent the message from the ad to the landing page, the better you are going to be.

This landing page will offer something of value, which could be a number of things. You could offer a whitepaper, video, free trial, free download, PDF, training course, or demo; the opportunities and options are endless.

The purpose here is to get visitors to micro-commit by giving you their contact information in exchange for what it is you have in value for them that will help solve the problem.

How much information you ask for depends greatly on the purpose of this micro-commitment. It can be as simple as asking for an email address, all the way to providing a name, email, phone, username, and password.

The amount of information you ask for in relation to what you are offering is important. It may be difficult to justify getting a full record (name, email, address, phone, etc.) when you are giving away only a simple PDF document. Keep the commitment in line with what you are offering.

On this landing page, be sure to keep the distractions to a

minimum. One clear path is usually your best bet, so don't give visitors the options to go someplace else by having a bunch of links or multiple offers available.

Onto the next step — your visitors find your information enticing and want more. They give you the information you ask for.

Upon clicking the button, they are then taken to another landing page. This time with a different purpose, another commitment, but now it's in the form of a sale.

Of course you want to deliver what it is that you promised them on the first page. This can be done through sending an email, or as part of the next page.

There are many different strategies for what to offer after someone makes the first step micro-commitment. Unfortunately, since many people are so afraid to actually "sell" something to these new leads, they don't actually present them with anything to buy at this point.

Instead of presenting them with an offer, they simply say, "Thanks, here is the info you requested."

When do you think it would be easier to ask for a sale?

In an email after visitors have had a chance to digest the free information?

Immediately after visitors have made a small commitment?

I hope you answered "B." Sure, email follow-up is great, but right after you get a small commitment is the hottest time to ask for a sale.

Your visitors are thinking about it, they are searching for a solution, they asked for more information by requesting your lead magnet, they are ready to buy, or at least a percentage of them are ready.

Now what you offer here and how much you charge greatly depends on your market.

A good rule of thumb is that what you offer builds on what you offered in step 1 of your funnel — the more complete solution to the problem.

As far as price, giving your visitors a lower barrier to entry here to get yet another commitment is crucial.

I have seen funnels offer anything from $7 reports to $300 video training courses and literally everything in between. This, again, depends on the market, what you are offering, and your audience.

The main point here is to, again, solve the problem and have enough value to justify paying to get the solution.

You want your visitors to commit to buying something from you even if the price tag is lower, as it is much easier to sell something at a higher price to an existing customer than it is to sell to a colder lead on average.

Pro Tip: After becoming a lead, 2-5% of people seeing this offer should take it, but pay close attention to your numbers to make it work in your favor.

Now you have a percentage of people who said "yes" to your

offer who bought it. Now what?

Remember, I just said it is easier to sell a higher-ticket offer to an existing customer. Plus, earlier I mentioned one-click upsells.

Well, now is the time to do that.

The new customer just clicked submit on your checkout page. You need to now present them with a special one-time only offer.

Now in this step, you can keep it simple or make it as complex as you want with downsells and multiple upsells. Again, this greatly depends on your market and how aggressive you want to be.

The point of this special one-time offer is to present a complimentary add-on to what your new customer just purchased for a higher price.

A good rule of thumb is to offer something that is 2X the price of what your customer just bought. But the key is to make it a truly special offer. You can do this in the form of a discount typically.

If the product normally sells for $300, you would want to offer it in your one-time offer to new customers at something like $150.

This makes it irresistible to the new customer, and as a result, we shoot for 25-45% of people to take advantage of this offer as our benchmark.

I have consistently seen 73% on a particular funnel, which is actually pretty incredible.

As you have seen in a pattern here, it all depends on your goal from a numbers perspective.

Upsells help offset ad costs and bring up your initial customer value, making your campaign more profitable quicker.

Now there are many different elements and techniques you can use from here: email follow-up, webinars, coaching, and pretty much an endless opportunity to sell additional products and provide value to your new customers.

SEVEN
Conversion Optimization Deep Dive

"Testing is the single most profitable skill any online marketing should master." ~ Eric Graham

When looking at conversion rate optimization (CRO), it is important to have a plan in place. The plan will help you discover bottlenecks and leverage points, which will lead to the 2X-10X growth you are looking for.

In this chapter we are going to go deep into our main 5-point process, which is used regardless of the market, site, or audience, to discover these growth points.

It is still amazing that even large companies, spending millions per month, don't stay on top of their testing and don't have a plan like this in place.

We consulted with a company recently that was spending over

$75,000,000 per year on advertising yet it hadn't tested its landing pages in a year.

With just a few simple tweaks and a plan like the following in place, the company could realize a huge increase in return on such a large investment.

When looking at CRO, the first step is to establish your baselines.

To do this, you look at several different areas and metrics. As we touched on earlier, you need to know your conversion rates, your EPC, CPC, and customer value, just to name a few.

Keep in mind that you have to look at your entire sales cycle and process as a whole. There are some instances when increasing the conversion rate on one element could actually decrease your revenue.

An example of this occurred on a campaign we were running for a client. The actual test proved to decrease the click-through slightly according to several goals, but the overall conversion rate to sale increased by more than 500%.

When looking, you need to pay attention to your visitor data from your favorite analytics tools. Have a video on the page? How long are people watching the video before leaving? How many people click-through to another page, what pages are they visiting, how long are they staying on each page, where are they clicking, how many are taking the desired action, where are they getting confused?

By looking at the data, you can determine the low hanging

fruit to begin plugging the holes in your marketing funnel.

An example of plugging the holes occurred with a client in the confectioner treats market. The client had a 3-step process in order to actually buy the offer. We found that a good chunk of people visiting the site were falling off on step 2.

To remedy this, we streamlined the actual checkout process, essentially removing one of the steps. The result was an increase of over 128% in actual orders.

What would an increase in 128% mean for your business? The opportunities for this type of growth are all over the place; sometimes you just need a second set of eyes on them in order to find them. The data and baselines will tell you pretty much everything you need to know; you just have to know where to look.

Install heatmap software, like crazy egg, to get better insights as to what your visitors are clicking on, what they are paying attention to, and what they aren't paying attention to.

Look at analytics data to see which pages are bringing the most engagement, where the majority of visitors go on your site, where they are falling off, and what areas need some attention.

A good example of a bottleneck is your checkout page. You may find by looking at the data that only a small percentage of people are actually making a purchase after landing on your checkout page.

This of course is a big problem and is actually not that uncommon. Many companies focus on getting people to the checkout page but neglect the actual checkout page.

This is go-time and prime opportunity to dramatically increase your results.

A few options here are to continue the selling process. Give your visitors the benefits of the product they are going to purchase again. Highlight your guarantee. Use strong calls-to-action to tell visitors what to do next. Leverage proof and security elements.

Don't just throw up a page with credit card fields and hope people buy. Keep selling them throughout the entire process, including the checkout page.

The vital information is right in front of you, and the first major step to an optimization plan is to get a good handle on what you are dealing with. Let the data be your guide.

Step number 2 in the process of your conversion optimization plan is actually a pretty important one that most people don't actually do as often as they should.

If you have an existing customer base, it is actually quite simple, so there is no excuse for you not to do it. It comes in the form of surveying the market— sending a simple survey out to the existing market to find out why they bought, what they liked about the product, and even more importantly what they didn't like about the process and product.

Sometimes, the bad news is better than anything you can possibly think of. This information helps you realize where you are falling short and gives you the insights as to where you need to look in order to improve.

Your customers are the best resources for telling you how well you are doing and where you can improve.

Many companies simply don't want to hear the "bad" news about their product or service. Yes, it can be painful to actually see it because we don't like that people may dislike us.

But this information is crucial if want to be better. This feedback allows you to steer the business ship and deliver better quality service for the price to your customers.

Don't be afraid of a little negative feedback. Plus, providing un-happy customers with a place to vent their frustrations in private will keep them from going public with it, which can be bad for your reputation overall.

The third step is to look at a competitive analysis. Now, typically we don't care much about competition but often times your competitors can give us key insights into the market that you normally wouldn't see — key leverage points in marketing funnels, traffic, and the entire process that can be leveraged in your own efforts to increase your results.

Now, before you say anything, we most certainly are not saying to "copy" your competition. We are simply looking for strategies or other leverage points to set our own campaigns up for success.

What are they doing right, and more importantly, where are they lacking?

A recent example of where this proved to be extremely valuable was with a highly recognized brand in the home loan lending space that was having trouble getting its display advertising campaign to be profitable.

After digging in, we found one competitor and actually one preferred partner that were spending 2 to 3 times as much on display ads and actually had more than 40 times the market impact than our client did — 40X fewer results because of the strategy this company was using. The company was giving up a good chunk of profits in the form of commissions to its preferred partner advertising to the same people.

The analysis has given this company the insights to take things in a slightly different direction to actually make its campaign profitable.

This definitely gave the company some leverage it might not have realized otherwise and it most definitely saved the company millions of dollars.

The fourth step in our conversion optimization plan is to take a long hard look at our own sites, funnel, and process to look for leverage points.

Ask yourself, "What am I doing right and where am I lacking?"

"Are there some elements that I'm missing?"

Often times, the littlest item could yield big returns, for example, having an extra field in your form that serves no purpose.

In the case of one particular campaign we were working on in the enterprise SaaS space, there was a form field asking, "How did you hear about us?" It wasn't necessary to have this form field, as tracking showed exactly where people were coming from. The result was friction.

Removing that single form field improved conversions 70.1%.

Remove friction to increase conversions:

We all know that the fewer roadblocks you have in the way of your prospects becoming customers, the better off you are going to be.

You want to provide your prospects with the quickest pain-free path to give you money that you can. This means simple instructions, clear communication, and every possible option to complete the buying decision.

In the case of one of our clients, her prospects were instructed to sign up for a free account, which included choosing their username and password. Normally, you would think that is pretty self-explanatory, as just about every website these days has some kind of "login" function.

Well, in online marketing, we don't assume anything, and the more places you can "help" the prospect through the process, the better off you are going to be in the long run. Basically, you need to—for lack of a better term—"dumb it down" for your prospects and treat your prospects/process as if they have never done anything like it before.

As you will see in this section, helping your prospects through the process can dramatically increase the conversion results you are looking for.

Like I mentioned, this client was asking the prospect to select login details.

Username: **?** [

Password: **?** [

To remove some of the friction and to help our client, we decided to test a simple "hover" next to the form field where customers select their usernames and passwords.

As you can see in the image, we added the "?" which hovered to messages that read the following:

Username: *"Please choose a username for your account. We recommend something short and easy to remember. Keep in mind that your username will be visible in your referral links, so it is important that you choose something that you want to be seen."*

Password: *"Please choose a password for your free account setup. We recommend a password between 8 and 12 characters long containing both letters and numbers. Be sure to write down your password so you can*

remember it when logging into your
account. "

We ran a simple A/B test with one page containing the "hovers" and the other page without.

You wouldn't think it would make that much of a difference, but remember that in marketing we can't assume ANYTHING.

In this case, thinking that it wouldn't make a big difference would have proved to be a BIG mistake.

The "?" with the messages explaining what we wanted the prospects to do increased the conversion rate on people signing up for the account, not by a little, but by a whopping 76%, 76.77% to be exact.

The page without the "?" converted at 3.75% while the page containing the help fields converted at 6.63%.

That is a HUGE increase in conversions from a change that took very little effort to implement.

The moral of the story here is that you need to remove friction. In this case, it was what we wanted prospects to do with the their usernames and passwords. The more friction you can remove from your entire sales process, the more opportunity you give your website visitors to complete the processes you want them to complete, whether it is become a lead by filling out the form, filling out the order form, buying additional products in a one-step upsell process, or buying additional products as a repeat customer.

Take a long hard look at your process and see if there are

friction points that can be removed, or if there are any possibilities to add a little "help."

Either way, test it and see what results you can produce.

Are you showcasing proof of your product or service?

We added a simple banner to the top of the page on one client's campaign that simply read, "15,753 Happy Students" and as a result increased sales conversions 27.3%.

Another example was on a checkout page. We added some Facebook chatter screenshots from the client's fan page and it increased sales conversions over 200%.

Your potential leads and customers want to know that what they are buying is what you say it is. They need that warm and fuzzy feeling that others have experienced great results from said product or service.

Another side of that is to showcase major media mentions, reviews, or any other proof you can leverage in your message.

Is your sales message congruent throughout the entire process, meaning are you highlighting the benefits, proof, and other sales elements throughout the entire buying process?

If you aren't, you are missing out on some major improvement.

Each page in the process allows for another chance to prove they are making the right decision and will get the desired result from the product.

Many companies focus on the initial message and fail to continue selling, which results in lackluster results.

Are you maximizing the space above the fold of the page? Studies have shown that you have less than 3 seconds to capture the attention of your visitors, and that number is shrinking.

Above the fold of the page is prime real estate in the online world, and if you are cluttering that area up with unneeded information, you are missing opportunities to increase your results.

You know those fancy sliders people use on their home pages--the ones with multiple images showcasing key elements of their product? Well, multiple tests have shown that these pretty elements actually decrease conversions by 30-50%.

Any movement on the page is distracting to visitors, causing them to bounce. Instead, focus on a single static image with a strong benefit-driven headline, bullet points loaded with benefits, a strong call-to-action, and some proof, if possible.

Your visitors need to understand what your product or service is, what it will do for them, and what to do next, all within a few seconds. Make use of this prime real estate to drive up your conversions.

Is your page mobile optimized?

Now this is a big one with the ever growing mobile market. Even if you don't get a ton of mobile traffic, at least make sure your page is mobile responsive. Google weighs mobile ready pages more heavily in pretty much all aspects of their algorithms, so make sure your page is mobile responsive.

The purpose of taking a look at your own site pages and elements is we want to find all of the leverage points we can in this step, as it will set us up perfectly for the next step in our master plan.

So now that we have our baseline metrics, our survey results, our competitive analysis, and our own internal leverage points listed, it is time to move onto step number 5 in the process.

Our split-testing plan of attack or step 5 in our process.

This is where the real magic happens, and in a later chapter, you will actually see the magic of continuous improvement in action.

In this step, we want to take all of our new found knowledge and come up with a list of things to split-test, starting with the low hanging fruit.

Based on the data, sometimes incremental changes are all that is needed to start. In some cases you may need to redesign the entire page to incorporate all the changes and split-test it against your control. Once you find a "big swing" winner, you can then do incremental testing to increase it further.

When looking at a campaign, it is good to start with at least 5 test ideas with 3-10 variations of each. This is usually a good starting point. Having any more than this is just a waste of time. As you begin testing, you will find that the plan often changes based on the data, and you come up with more important tests along the way.

The number of variations you begin testing with really depends on the amount of traffic and conversions you have as your baseline.

Too many variations with too little traffic can lead to tests taking too long to get significant results.

We typically like to run at least 25 conversions per variation before we ever begin taking a serious look at the results and making changes.

If you can't get that many conversions in a week or two on each variation, you may want to limit the number of variations.

The other side of the coin applies as well. If you have a significant amount of daily traffic and conversions, running more variations is feasible.

To take this part a step further, we may decide to run tests on only a percentage of the overall traffic, sometimes 30%-50%.

This is done for a couple of reasons, with the main one being that if for some reason we have a big loser as a variation, it only affects a smaller percentage of the overall traffic and doesn't compromise any other results.

Other areas where you can improve conversions?

There are dozens of areas where you can improve conversions and it isn't just limited to the obvious landing pages and sales pages.

Every area where visitors engage also includes opportunities for improvements.

Have a blog?

What do you show in the sidebar of your posts? How about the signature message at the bottom of each post?

Test out different call-to-actions, banners, and opt-in forms.

You use your content to bring value to the market and bring people to your site, so pay attention to how they interact and place the proper message in front of them, which leads them down the path to a desired action you want.

Have a checkout page where you ask for credit card information to order? If you are selling online you need to pay extra close attention to these pages, as some of the biggest opportunities for improvement are on these pages.

Pay close attention to how many steps you have in the checkout process. If you have too many, you could be dramatically decreasing your conversions.

Test progress bars, hero shot images of your product, benefits of purchasing, video, proof, and secure seals to reduce abandon cart rate.

You can also test using exit warnings to keep people on the page. After all, you spent a good bit of time, energy, and possibly money to get people to this page. Now is the time to push them over the edge. What good does it do if 90% of the people who land on that page don't make a purchase?

Are you asking visitors to choose what type of credit card they want to pay with? Try having your cart automatically identify the card instead of having them choose. We have found this to improve conversions 10%-30%.

Be sure you highlight the types of cards you accept. You may even want to give them more options to pay. If you only accept Visa or Mastercard, try adding Discover and American Express to see if that increases your conversions. The increase in sales can far outweigh the slightly higher fees.

Have a suite of products in your online store? Have a list of best-sellers? Try making it obvious by highlighting a best-sellers section in your menu. We have found in various tests that doing this can increase site engagement 40% or more increase sales 20% or more.

Are you sending email to your customers or prospects? Test subject lines, message type, content, call-to-actions, and sequence of the message to increase engagement.

I think you get the idea. Every area where you "touch" someone in your target audience has an opportunity for improvement. Whether you are optimizing for engagement, leads, or sales, look at where you can improve the experience for your visitors. The result is worth the extra effort you put in.

EIGHT

Testing Mistakes And How To Avoid Them

"A person who never made a mistake never tried anything new."
~ Albert Einstein

You say you are testing and working on improving your conversion rates, but most likely you are making some mistakes. Mistakes as in the quote that opened this chapter are sometimes par for the course but the more help you can get to avoid them the better.

After thousands of tests, we have boiled it down to these 4 common mistakes people make when looking at conversion optimization.

1. False Positives

You have a 6 way A/B test running, looking to improve some engagement on your site by changing the headlines. Quickly you see a clear winner, but you stay the course gathering more data to make sure you have a clear winner. The test reaches 95% conclusive, and thinking you really have stumbled upon something great, you decide to run with the changes only to be left scratching your head when the increase wasn't an increase at all.

What happened?

That my friend is what we like to call a false positive. Everything looks great but other factors played a role in the outcome of the test, such as people, other steps of the funnel, etc.

To remedy this, cut the losers and retest the winning variable against the control again in order to confirm you truly have a winner. This will take a little extra time but it will be worth it.

2. Not knowing when to say when

We see it all too often. You setup a test but it seems to take forever to reach conclusive results. None of the variables seem to be showing much promise, but you still sit on the test waiting for it to magically turn into an improvement. Plenty of data is being collected but there is still no true winner.

What we recommend here is to cut ties with the test and turn your focus to elements that could yield more of an impact. It is okay to fold your hand on tests if they aren't showing improvement and focus on other elements that will.

For example, we had been sitting on a test for 2 weeks with

one client and the stats just didn't seem to be changing much. There were plenty of conversions on each of the variables but still no clear winner. So we decided to stop that test and turn our focus to other places where we could see some distinct improvement.

3. Testing too many small elements

Oh, believe me, there is a time and a place for incremental changes that can yield big results. We have loads of those case studies. But sometimes what you need is an entirely new look and feel.

For the sake of example, we had a client campaign that was getting dismal results on its lead generation. We tested a completely new landing page, and the results were over a 300% increase on one traffic source.

Once you make the big change, start testing backwards, working on the incremental changes to dial in your conversion rates even further.

4. Not sticking with it

This is a big one. You run a few tests, see some improvements, then turn your attention to something else. In order to have full control over your conversion rate optimization, you need to continually be testing. Markets change, people change, so your marketing efforts should change too.

Even the slightest improvement is great, and we are firm believers in compounding conversions, the slight edge on continuous improvement. Sometimes, you will have big winners and sometimes small ones, but it is important that you keep at it, as it will pay big dividends in the long run.

Bonus: Wrong focus

Thought we would throw out a little bonus element here. For the sake of your testing, you need to make sure you are focusing on the RIGHT metrics, as not all improvements will make you more money.

Instead of focusing on the single page conversion rate, keep your focus on your actual earnings per click and customer value. After all, those are the elements that drive out profit.

All other elements should lead to the bigger goal, which is an increase in customer value. It is not always a fast path but it is a rewarding one.

NINE

Conversion Optimization Checklist

"We don't assume anything and test everything."

~ Dean Strickler

Through thousands of split-tests and hundreds of campaigns, we have boiled it down to the top 20 areas we find to have the most impact on your conversion goals. Here we go…

Headline:

Attention is a scarce resource. If you don't grab your visitors' attention within seconds and compel them to read on, watch your video, or continue to the next step in your buying process, everything you put on the rest of the page doesn't matter because frankly, no one will see it.

Studies have shown, as mentioned earlier, that you have as little as 3 seconds to grab the attention of your visitors, and that amount of time is likely to become even less. This starts with the ad itself, of course, but carries over to your actual landing page.

Just think of all the ads you see on a daily basis with basic browsing alone. Everyone is clawing for your attention, so it is important that you grab your visitors' attention and suck them into looking at more of your page and offering.

An example of a recent test that proved well was with an ecommerce client.

On the client's best-sellers page, the headline on the page simply read "Best-Sellers." We tested a bunch of headlines on that page and the winner, which provided a 68.7% lift in the click-through rate to the checkout page, was "Shop Our Best-Selling Products."

Not a huge change to the page, but the change produced a big lift in engagement.

Often, we say the headline could be the most important element. Some people even think we are silly for putting so much emphasis on the headline at times, but they don't think we are silly when they see the results.

Nine times out of ten, testing headlines has proven to have a big impact on conversion rates—an improvement of anywhere from 27% to 118% by simply swapping out a tired headline with a catchy benefit-driven one.

Pricing:

What if twice as many people bought your product at a 10% lower price? What if raising your prices actually attracted MORE buyers? The phrase "You never know until you test" has never been more true than when it comes to pricing.

Now when testing pricing, you have to be careful. Be sure you watch your average customer value and upsell take rates if you have upsells. Pricing can have a negative effect and actually make you less money even though you sell more stuff on the front end.

For example, we once had two similar products at the same time that were priced at about $39. We decided to test $19.95 and $29 for the price on each of them.

The result was that $19.95 actually doubled the amount of sales and had almost no impact on the upsell take rate, and with the sister product, the $19.95 price point cut the conversion rate in half and dramatically decreased the upsell take rate.

The $29 price point actually tanked conversions in both cases.

In the online marketing game, you often see prices ending in 9 or 7, such as $7, $17, $19, $27, $47, $77, etc., because sometime long ago someone claimed that having your pricing structured this way would boost conversions. We have never seen official proof that this works, though. But we have tested many different types of pricing, and the answer? Well, it all depends on what you are selling and who you are selling it to.

When testing pricing, we find that it is better to test a broad spectrum of pricing as opposed to incremental changes. For example, test $99 vs $299 instead of $99 vs $89.

Of course this depends on your product or service. You may find that a much higher price not only makes you more money but more people also want to buy it.

One of the surefire ways to make more money is to charge more, and often, it is that easy.

But there are also cases when even the slightest change can destroy your conversions. A campaign we were working on a short time ago showed this to be completely true. The client had a low margin product so even the slightest increase in price could make a huge difference in his bottom line.

The client's product was priced at $12, which proved to be a fantastic price point for customer acquisition. We decided to test just $.99 cents more, making the price $12.99. The result? Sales flat-lined.

Essentially, there is a reason that pricing is toward the top of the list, as it plays a vital role in your sales and marketing. Test it out for yourself.

Call-to-action:

To maximize your conversions, every page on your site should be designed to get visitors to take one specific action—an action that will move them one step further in the buying process.

It could be to join your mailing list, proceed to your online store, add an item to their shopping cart, or fill in their credit card details to complete their order.

Every page is a chance to continue the selling process. In this case, a good rule of thumb is don't assume your website visitors know what to do. Rather, you need to tell them what to do.

It could be as simple as stating "Click The Add To Cart Button Below Now." But by telling your visitors what you want them to do next, it leaves less margin of error.

As an example, there was this particular client who was working to put people into a "free" membership in order to be upgraded to a paying customer through his sales funnel.

On the client's landing page, he had a video explaining all the benefits of becoming a member. And in addition to this video was a form that asked for a username, password, name, and email—all the standard stuff—including a call-to-action, telling visitors what he wanted them to do.

The original call-to-action read something like this: "Fill Out The Form To Claim Your Free Account."

We ran a simple A/B split-test on the landing page on just the call-to-action.

Below is a screenshot of the actual call-to-action we tested against the original.

Fill Out The Form Below To Get Instant Access 100% FREE Now!

Name: [▲]

Email: [   ]

As you can see it was just a minor change of only a few words. But the addition of the phrase "100% Free" made a dramatic difference in the actual number of people who submitted the form.

A staggering 158% MORE people signed up for their free account—158.23% increase to be exact.

Instead of just under 6% of this client's visitors signing up, he now had over 15% of his web visitors becoming members. This was just from ONE page on his site. It doesn't take into account all the other pages in his funnel that were optimized over a few months—just one slight change to the call-to-action made the world of difference.

Try it out for yourself. Look at all the places you could potentially "tell" people what to do and find ways to convey that message better. You may find it makes a big difference.

CTA Button Design:

When you're visiting a website, it's hard to imagine that your decision to buy or not to buy could be influenced so strongly by something as arbitrary as the shape, color, or size of a button.

But believe it or not, test after test has shown that button design can make a big difference in your conversions, from what the button says, to its color and size. All of these factors play a roll.

Color has been scientifically tied to emotion, and emotions have a direct correlation with buying decisions. People tend to tie their buying decisions to their emotions—usually to either avoid pain or gain pleasure.

Nothing is more irritating than loading a perfectly good website and seeing the out-of-the-box yellow gradient button slap me in the face.

Not only does that tell me that the site owner doesn't care about his or her conversions, but that site owner obviously isn't testing, which in our book is a big no-no.

We had one particular client for whom we did a BUNCH of testing, particularly on the button. The landing page was pretty simple in design so one of the key elements was the button.

This was a free offer to get a free membership.

The original button was as pictured—a yellow gradient button with navy blue text that said, "Give Me My Free System!"

We tested not only the color but also just about every wording combo you could think of that made sense with the offer, from "I Want My Free System" to "I'll Take It," and while testing all the different wording options, we also tested the color of the buttons, including the highly used yellow gradient button, the orange gradient, and of course the red gradient.

The result?

The yellow button actually got crushed in every test we ran with it, no matter what the button actually said. The orange gradient came in a close second.

The winning combo, which actually came as a huge surprise, was the red gradient button with white text that simply said "Free Instant Access."

How much did it win by you may be asking…

The red "Free Instant Access" button converted at 154.55% better than the control in this case.

The numbers actually looked pretty close in just about all tests that were run. What the button said actually moved the needle quite a bit as well but not nearly as much as the color of the button.

Now not all button tests are going to increase conversions by over 150%, but in almost all cases you will find the button plays a big part in how well your site converts.

Test what makes sense to you.

A simple click and a dramatic increase:

Say a prospect is on your site taking in all of the sales goodness you have presented.

The prospect is seeing the benefits, foaming at the mouth, and reaching for his or her credit card to buy your amazing product or service.

But there is something holding the prospect back from going through with the purchase.

There have been many tests performed on whether you should have prospects click on a button to be taken to your secure order page or you should just show them the form right there on the page.

Since we don't assume anything is going to convert better, we did what we do best and tested it out.

We had a client who was using a video to sell her solution, which in this case was a training system.

At a particular time in the video, the video was coded to show a button that contained a clear call-to-action to make a purchase. The prospect would then have to click the button to be directed to the secure checkout page.

What we did was setup a test that had the checkout form show up on the same page as the video so the prospect wouldn't have to click a button to be taken to the secure checkout page, thus eliminating a step in the process.

The result from this little test actually proved our assumption correct, which was that skipping the "click" step would increase conversions.

In this case skipping the "click" increased the conversions 43.59%, meaning that if we had 1,000 unique visits to the sales page, the "click" version at the 2.3% conversion rate would have had 23 people order, while the on-page checkout version would have 33 orders.

That is a huge increase from making one small change.

If you are having people click to be taken to your order form, we encourage you to try this little trick out for yourself. You might just be surprised at how much of an impact it has on your conversions.

Benefits Copy:

Compelling copy is your most effective weapon for boosting conversions and dominating your competition. In sales and marketing, words have massive power.

A skilled copywriter can use those words to dig deep into the core desires and emotions of your visitors to get them to buy what you're selling.

Make sure your copy is benefit driven. Highlight benefits over features as potential customers don't care about the features as much as they care about the benefits or end results.

Page Style:

The look and feel of your site goes a long way towards establishing trust and conveying the personality of your brand.

But what converts when it comes to page styles is often counter-intuitive.

In many industries, "ugly" pages that look like they were put together in an afternoon out-convert beautifully designed, professional-looking pages.

Often, companies go for aesthetics over conversions, which can be catastrophic to their conversion rate.

Now we are not saying to just go throw up an ugly page because "ugly pages convert better." We are saying that the layout and style of your pages play a big role and "pretty" doesn't always win.

Thanks to all the tools available to create pages easily, marketers tend to follow trends. So-and-so is using this style page so it must work—this could be the case, but each business and product is different so you need to find what works for you.

Here is an example of that.

We know you have seen them, the simple landing pages with the full background images.

You know the ones that have just a simple headline, maybe an email only form, or a button that opens up the form in a lightbox?

The background images vary of course, but almost anywhere we turn we see them.

But since they first became popular, we have been posing the question, "Are they actually converting better than other more traditional styles of landing pages?" To figure this out, we did what we do best and ran a test to find out.

Don't just assume something will work without testing it to prove it will work.

We have said this before and we will say it again: just because something works for one person or offer that doesn't mean it is going to work for you and yours. If you aren't testing and optimizing, you are on a slippery slope leading to a disaster.

One of our clients was running a standard video landing page on a new offer he had just created. So we decided to test via simple A/B testing to see if the full background image page using a similar headline and call-to-action would increase the conversion rate like so many people had been raving about.

The result was the full background page actually decreased the conversion rate on the offer by 7.12%.

Now 7.12% might not seem like much, but a decrease is a decrease and things compound.

If we plug the 6.31% and the 5.86% conversion rates into our 10,000 visitors and $10 lead value from the chart above, here is what it would look like:

Control (6.31%):
631 leads @ $10 per lead =
$6,310
Full Background (5.86%):

586 leads @ $10 per lead =
$5,860

In this example, if we would have just assumed the full background page would convert better, we would have lost $450 in revenue for every 10,000 visitors we sent to the site.

You have to find out what works for you—a page layout that fits your brand and product, and the type of traffic you are driving to that particular page. One size doesn't always fit all.

Showcasing your product with images:

During some client testing we found something really interesting that we thought would be good to share with you.

It all stems from showcasing your product during the checkout process.

This particular client sells confectioner treats, such as chocolates, candies, and others.

They also have a monthly membership tied to it.

While looking for friction points in the sign-up process and things to test, we noticed the client didn't have any product images on the pricing page. So we did what we do best and tested that out.

Right below the pricing table—in this case, a monthly, quarterly, and yearly billing plan—we added a simple image of some of the product (see an example below). We tested multiple images to see if they held any weight when it came to conversions.

The result from this test was nothing short of amazing.

As a result of adding some "showcase" images of the product, the conversion rates skyrocketed.

CONVERSION RATE CONVERSION RATE ERROR	IMPROVEMENT
5.43% (±4.66)	---
10.89% (±6.11)	+100.4%

There was an over 100% increase in sales conversion from ONE simple image.

The results of this test led to us thinking of other ways we could showcase products in different ways around the site to increase conversions.

So far, it has proven to be successful in all areas of the site. PLUS, we tested a similar philosophy with another client who sells completely different products, this time tracking for revenue per visitor/customer.

VARIATION	REVENUE VISITORS	REVENUE PER VISITOR REVENUE ERROR	IMPROVEMENT
Original	521.97 234	2.2306 (±0.2858)	---
Vertical Box 1	531.99 244	2.1803 (±0.2736)	-2.3%
Vertical Box 2	801.00 221	3.6244 (±0.4779)	+62.5%
Lip Gloss 1	1010.95 273	3.7031 (±0.4393)	+66.0%

In this case, it improved revenue per customer over 66%—can't complain about that one bit.

I encourage you to go out there and see if there are ways you can showcase your product during your sales process to see what impact it has on your conversion rates.

Navigation:

Most people think usability is about making their site easy to get around for visitors. But when it comes to increasing conversions, a more usable site is usually one that gives visitors fewer options, with a clearer path of action.

If your goal is to convert visitors into buyers, you need to lead them step-by-step through the buying process.

Giving them too many options will encourage them to meander around your site before losing interest and clicking away.

Guarantee:

As consumers we love to keep our options open for as long as possible, and the commitment to buying products means that your customer will lose the freedom to spend that money on other things.

A strong guarantee reduces that fear of loss by letting the

customer know that she can always change her mind later. It also reassures her that if anything goes wrong with the order she is protected.

Smart online retailers know that the increase in sales from a strong guarantee usually outweighs the small increase in returns that might come from it.

Now there is much debate about whether to offer a guarantee or not. Some people say that by offering a guarantee you are not attracting the right kinds of customers, which will lead to problems down the road, whereas other people swear by guarantees.

We come from the angle that it depends on what you are selling. But more times than not, if you are selling consumer products, a money-back guarantee makes a world of difference.

Take, for instance, a campaign we worked on a few years ago. The company had a 90-day money-back guarantee, which proved to be great for the company and its sales. In looking for ways to improve, we suggested testing a 1-year guarantee to see how that moved the needle.

As a result, sales came close to doubling, while the refund rate only went up about 3%.

We have found that the majority of people who are going to ask for a refund do so within the first 90 days anyway Of course the rare occasion exists in which people will find an excuse to ask for a refund later on in the cycle. My personal favorite excuse was "My daughter got kidnapped, so I need my $39 back from over a year ago."

True or not, there will always be those people who want to get refunded later, but the benefits should far outweigh the negatives.

We had one client who for the longest time didn't state a money-back guarantee in any of her marketing.

While dialing in a paid advertising campaign, we wanted to see just how important having a money-back guarantee was to the client's conversion rate in her particular market, so we added a simple 30-day guarantee to the sales page.

The result was an increase in conversions by 26%—a pretty good increase in conversions from adding just some simple language to the sales page.

The philosophy here is simple, as stated earlier. Having this simple guarantee makes visitors/prospects feel all warm and fuzzy and confident in their buying decision. They know that if they aren't satisfied they can get their money back. There really isn't a much more powerful option to remove friction and risk in your marketing.

Of course you need to stand behind your guarantee no matter what you offer.

Here is another cool case study from a different client involving refund periods having a positive impact.

This client was in a relatively small niche online. Since he started his business back in 2008, he had always offered a lifetime guarantee. He was extremely confident in his product and it was one thing that set him apart from everyone else in the market. He was the ONLY one offering such a guarantee.

He has found similar results in the refund rate. The majority of people who refund do so within the first 90 days, with less than 1% refunding after 1 year from their date of purchase.

In fact, after thousands of customers, he has only had 2 people refund after 1 year.

How long is your money-back guarantee?

In marketing, it is important to remove as much risk and friction on the part of your prospects as you can. One of the most common ways to do this is to offer a money-back guarantee.

Now there are different methods of implementing a money-back guarantee. You can offer things like your standard 30-, 60-, 90-day guarantees. Another couple options are offering a 1-year or lifetime guarantee. Some companies even go as far as offering double money-back.

No matter which way you go with your guarantee, it has become a pretty common practice.

Will increasing your refund period increase your results? Does it set you apart from the rest of your market?

Test it out for yourself to see just what kind of impact it can have on your business.

Trust:

The old saying goes that people buy from people they know, like, and trust. People flock to Amazon.com to buy pretty much anything you can imagine.

Even though anyone can list their products on Amazon, the trust is there.

When looking at your sales funnel, think of ways you can increase the trust level with your prospects and website visitors.

Sometimes this takes time as well, dripping content on them via email or constantly staying on the front of their minds through remarketing.

Other ways to build trust is to piggyback off of other larger brands or trade publications. This also ties into proof elements.

If you are featured in a major trade publication, showcase that. Do you have thousands of happy customers? Showcase how many. Do you have glowing feedback and reviews from past customers? Make sure new people see those. Have you won any awards or are you a best-selling author on the topic? Yep, you guessed it, feature all of that.

The more you can instill elements of trust in your marketing, the better off you will be. Of course there could be some instances when this doesn't help, but 9 times out of 10, it does.

One little trick we have used multiple times is on the checkout page. At a former company, we tested a video on that page that highlighted why we were so awesome.

"We have produced the best-selling XYZ for going on 10 years now with over 65,000 customers in 26 different countries. I just wanted to make sure you knew that we stand behind all of our products 100% and

have a fabulous support team available
to answer any questions you may have.
To reach us you can call 888.555.1234
or by going to
www.mysite.com/support.
    We are excited to serve you, and
your satisfaction is important to us.
All you have to do now is fill out the
100% secure order form on this page
to continue."

Or something to that effect. The result was a 30% decrease in cart abandonment rate. Our results improved by showcasing just a little proof as well as making sure customers understood that we truly cared about them.

Trust Seals:

Entering your credit card information online is a scary thing, at least for the average consumer. Even with a well-established company, people are afraid of leaked information, identity theft, and fraud.

One way to help give your visitors the warm and fuzzy feeling of doing business with you is to highlight their safety through trust seals and other secure images.

Of course if you are accepting credit cards, you have a secure site, so showcasing the trust seal from your SSL certificate could pay big dividends.

There are also dozens of different third-party seals you can use to increase the security and credibility. We have seen the seals increase conversions anywhere from 30% to 150%.

It all depends on what you showcase and where.

Social Proof Elements:

Third-party opinions about your product are often more credible than your own claims. Social proof elements are the testimonials, media quotes, celebrity endorsements, and "as seen on" media logos that boost your credibility and authority to your visitors.

Since a lot of these elements are easy to fake, the more "real" you can make them, the better. If you don't have these elements, don't make them up just so you have them. Visitors can see through a 'fake' a mile away. Plus, that is just unethical business and marketing.

Here is a good case study demonstrating just how powerful proof elements can be:

We were optimizing a client's sales process and noticed she the pages of the funnel were lacking in terms of having proof elements listed. The client was getting a TON of buzz on social media at the time so we thought we would test it out to see just what type of impact this "proof" element had on sales.

Up until this point, the client had a pretty basic order form. In this case, the order form loaded directly on the same page as the sales video.

We ran a simple A/B test here by adding a screenshot of all the buzz/comments happening on Facebook to the order form.

Note: We used a screenshot and NOT a live-feed of the comments. Feel free to test out the live-feed if you have a bunch of comments coming in to see if you can get a bigger boost.

So we tested the screenshot vs. not having any proof at all—nothing too fancy.

But what was fancy were the results that came in after a few days of running the test.

We saw a 289.52% increase in conversions from adding the testimonials in the sidebar of the order form. Talk about a WOW moment.

After this test, we looked for other places in the funnel where we could incorporate proof elements.

We added proof to the sales video, the landing pages, and even the upsell pages. The increase from placing proof on these other pages ranged from 12% to 33% increases, depending on the application.

If you have success stories or letters from raving fans, we HIGHLY recommend that you find places in your sales process to incorporate them. But all I ask is that you don't assume they will work and just add them haphazardly. Set up a test and get the visible proof of the impact they have.

You might be surprised at the results, as I know we have been surprised at such a big impact from such a small change.

Video Styles:

Video is an incredibly powerful conversion tool—it allows you to convey complex concepts in an easy-to-understand way and can be used to give the viewer an experience of your product that words and static images can't come close to.

Also, video gives you control over the sequence and the pace of your message so your visitors see and hear only what you want them to and when you want them to, thus allowing you to build a much more persuasive case for making a purchase.

If your page includes an explainer or sales video, changing the style of the video or of the video player can make a massive difference to your conversions.

In the video itself, adding animation to the text-only version or replacing a voiceover with a live video of an actor can be all you need to give you a boost in engagement.

And when it comes to the video player, you can change the look, feel, and functionality of the player to increase conversions.

For example, many tests have found that taking away the viewers' ability to scroll through the video—or, in some cases, even to pause it—have dramatically increased conversions.

Things to test: text vs. live, text vs. animated, controls vs. no controls, colors and fonts, and video size.

In some cases, we have seen the benefits of using video vs. not using video to increase conversions as much as 300%.

Here is a real-world example of what we mean when we say the size of the video makes a difference:

With video it seems to come down to more than just the great content, the style of your presentation, and even the graphics that surround your video. All these things are important, however, especially from a conversion optimization standpoint, but we wanted to answer the age old question: does size matter?

Get your mind out of the gutter; we are talking about video size.

Now when I say video size, I am talking about the physical display as seen on your page. Actual file sizes and formats is a brand new discussion.

So how does video size play a role in your conversion rate?

With one client, we had a VSL, or video sales letter, on a page that was quite large on screen. We did some recon and looked at the page on all screen sizes, including mobile, and noticed that the call-to-action below the video wasn't showing up on the majority of the screen sizes.

Quick note: You need to think like your visitor. You may have a big fancy monitor for your computer, and your page may look great on it, but many of your visitors may not have this luxury, especially with the increase in mobile use.

A pro tip to help you with this is to look at your analytics data and see the operating systems and browsers that most of your visitors are coming from and then optimize for that.

Armed with our new found knowledge of screen sizes and how the VSL looked, we decided to run a test to see how the size of the video changed the conversion rate.

We setup a basic A/B test using our favorite testing tool.

On the first page, we kept the video the normal size, obviously.

On the second page, we dropped the size of the video by 20%.

Again, like in most of the case studies we present here at Conversion Fanatics, simple changes often make the biggest difference.

So what was the result of our little experiment?

The video size, in this case, is Variation 1, which converted 239.47% BETTER than the larger video size.

Talk about a HUGE increase from just one small change.

The reason for such an increase was the smaller video would allow the call-to-action to be moved above the fold of the page, making for easier viewing on most devices and screen sizes.

We don't want our visitors to have to scroll down to take the desired action.

The smaller video solved this problem and of course as you can see increased the conversion rate from 1.16% to 3.95%.

So pay attention to how your visitors are viewing your sites and test out the size of the video for yourself, as you too might be surprised at the results.

Unique Landing Pages:

Every source of traffic is different, and if they all lead to the same page, you're losing out on sales. By adding custom landing pages for each source of traffic, your conversions can increase dramatically.

Think about it for a second. If you clicked on an ad that said: "Get Whiter Teeth in 10 seconds a week," you'd want to land on a page that gives you exactly that; you wouldn't want to go to the generic homepage of a dental products company where you'd have to scroll around to find teeth whitener.

Custom landing pages for each traffic source not only make your pages more RELEVANT and therefore more persuasive to your visitors, they also increase your visitors' trust in you.

You've made good on the promise of your ad and in your visitors' minds, which means you're more likely to deliver on other promises.

Things to test: set up custom landing pages to match each ad, each keyword, and each source of traffic.

You might want to go as far as customizing the headline by

merging data from the location of the visitor, to make it more personalized.

Additionally, each traffic source may have different requirements with regard to what it wants to see on your landing page, so having custom landing pages for each allows you to optimize further and cater your message to that specific audience. Plus, it makes tracking a campaign quite a bit easier.

Exit Pop-Up:

You know how some sites have that annoying box that pops up when you try to exit? Why do they do that? Usually because it increases sales.

A lot of companies are resistant to using exit-pops because they personally find them annoying, but if you can get a 20% sales boost by reaching out to people who are leaving your site anyway, would that be worth it?

Exit pops aren't appropriate on all sites but when used correctly, they can considerably boost your top line revenue.

We must say though that a lot of paid traffic media don't allow pop-up offers, so you have to decide the best place to use them. Sometimes, it is beneficial to use them deeper in your funnel, such as on your checkout page, which can be beneficial in reducing the abandoned cart rate.

Don't overuse pop-ups or exit intent warnings, be tactful.

Here is one real world way to use them: try and save some of the visitors that are trying to leave your site and entice them into taking that ever so popular desired action.

Even when trying to "save" some of the visitors, there are dozens of different methods you can implement. Here, we are only going to focus on one along with the amazing results achieved with such a simple change.

One of our clients had a 30-day trial offer. For just $1, you could try the entire membership for a full 30 days. This was positioned as a special ONE-TIME ONLY chance to get the special trial offer. If visitors came back later, they wouldn't get the option.

Conversion rates were good, but since we are always striving for more, they could have been better.

So we implemented an "exit warning" on the page that would warn exiting visitors that they wouldn't get another chance at the $1 trial if they left.

Wait! Are You Sure You Want To Go?

This is your one chance to give an upgraded apprentice level account a try for a full 30 days for only $1. Give yourself every advantage to make more money by upgrading today.

This is a one time only chance to give it a test drive before you buy. Once you close this window you will have to pay full price should you choose to upgrade.

Click Cancel to stay on this page or next to continue.

Now I know you have seen exit pop ups before—that is unless you don't spend even a minute looking at websites.

This one is a little different. Instead of taking the visitor to another page, this warning loads and keeps the visitor on the same page.

As you can see, there is nothing fancy about it—no fancy graphics or anything like that—just a simple script that loads some text, warning visitors that they will not have another chance to get the trial.

We ran a simple A/B test on this particular page. One page had the exit warning and the other did not.

The result?

There was a 31.82% improvement in conversions.

This means that almost 32% more people took the upgraded offer and took the trial.

What would your business do with 32% more customers? Would it help? I hope you are nodding your head in agreement.

There is actually more to this than just a "Trial" and an increase in conversions. The visitors were actually given more options to purchase.

The membership after the trial was $37 per month. Visitors were also given the chance to save $10 per month if they paid $27 that day and skipped the trial. Or, they also had the chance to buy out the entire year at an additional savings.

We knew that over 28% of the people took the $27 option (making more money on day one) and 15% of people took the yearly option (again, making more money on day 1).

In reality this 32% increase yielded quite a bit of extra revenue collected on day one for this particular business in addition to just the trial offers.

So there you have it—one simple way to INCREASE your

conversion rate by trying to save the visitors who are looking to leave your site.

Take it, try it, and as always test it.

Chat Support:

Why are so many visitors leaving your page without buying? It could be that they have a question about a tiny detail of your offer that's not answered by your sales page.

Once they leave your page, the chance of them eventually returning to make a purchase drops dramatically. By adding chat support, you can answer their questions and remove their objections right then and there so they can complete their purchase.

It will also give you valuable intel about what the most common objections are so you can overcome these objections elsewhere on your page.

You can also add chat support post-sale to increase customer retention, improve customer experience, and free up your phone support to deal with more complicated issues.

Phone Support:

There's nothing like a real live person to answer your questions and reassure you that you'll be taken care of.

Even if no one calls it, the presence of a phone number on your page can increase visitors' trust that your company is made up of real people who care about the experience visitors have.

Depending on how much traffic you have, you'll need to make

sure you have customer support reps on hand, create phone scripts, and put tracking systems in place.

There are lots of companies you can outsource this to, or you can do it in-house.

Things to test: add phone support to your site. Test different placements. Try toll-free as well as local numbers—as in local to the visitor. There are several ways to do this.

Take, for example, the short infomercials you see on TV for the latest gadgets. They always have a phone number as well as a website address.

Be sure to test the call-to-action with the phone number as well. A little trick to test with that is, "If Lines Are Busy Keep Calling." Saying this has been proven to dramatically increase conversion rates.

Urgency and Scarcity:

Visitors don't just need a reason to buy; they need a reason to buy NOW.

Once a visitor leaves your site, the chances that they'll be back to make a purchase drops dramatically.

Fear of missing out is a powerful motivator, and letting your visitors know that if they don't purchase soon they'll miss out on something often pushes them over the edge from "Maybe I'll buy it someday" to "I need to buy it NOW!"

You can easily do this with limited stock items by displaying exactly how many items you currently have in stock. Or, you can add bonuses or limited-time discounts.

Things to test: periodic discounts, limited time offers, and displaying the numbers of items remaining for limited stock (i.e. "3 left").

Remind your visitors of an upcoming event that makes ordering soon important (i.e. order in the next 12 hours to receive by Christmas/Valentine's Day etc.) Offer a limited time, or a limited quantity discount.

Now when we say *scarcity,* we don't mean to use false scarcity, such as "Only 17 Copies Left" when you are selling digital goods.

Instead, limit the number of copies at that particular price— sort of like a mini-sale.

But when using scarcity elements, be honest and true to your word. Don't just say you have a limited number of copies available at that price and then continue selling at that price.

If you say you are going to close down the page after X number of units sold, do it. It will go much further when selling later on, meaning when you say you are going to do something, you do it, and your customers grow to know you are true to your word.

A real world example of this in action occurred with a client who was running a closeout offer on a relatively expensive product, just shy of $1,000.

The client was discontinuing the product and planned on a 10-day closeout.

The client had ran the first 6 days of the plan at the normal price, which was selling relatively well, and the client had collected close to $45,000 in that 6-day period. For the last 4 days of the promotion, we decided to kick it up a notch.

We slashed the price in half, making it just shy of $500 for the same product that had sold hundreds of units at $1,000. We didn't worry much about devaluing it, as it wasn't going to be offered again.

The result was in the last 4 days we collected just shy of $100,000.

The urgency and scarcity factors were that it would never be offered again, the price was 50% off, and the doors were closing in 4 days.

Back-end Offers:

It's much harder and more expensive to acquire a new customer than it is to increase the value of an existing one. Once visitors have spent their first penny with you, they've made that important leap from prospect to customer.

That first sale is called a "front-end offer," and products available after that are called "back-end offers." Since you've done most of the heavy-lifting of acquiring them as customers, you're leaving a lot of money on the table if you stop making offers to them after their initial purchase.

Add back-end offers to increase your revenue with very little extra effort.

Things to test: special offer emails, webinars, affiliate offers, phone campaigns, and premium offers.

Upsells:

People tend to spend money in spurts: once they've opened their wallets and made that first purchase, they're in "buying mode."

By offering them the chance to spend more with you right after they place their order (during the checkout process after they submit their credit card info), you can easily double or triple the value of your customers.

An upsell is a special kind of backend offer that's made right after the point of purchase. Many shopping carts can be configured to allow buyers to add an upsell to their order with a single click (i.e. without having to reenter their credit card info).

Adding and integrating upsells is one of the highest leverage strategies you can implement.

Things to test: OTOs (one-time offers), escalating prices, loss leaders, downsells, accelerators, and done-for-you and premium offers.

The best place to start is to offer a complimentary product and offer it at a discount from what your customers could potentially buy it for on its own.

An example of this happened with a campaign that sold a product for under $40. Once customers submitted a credit card, they were shown a series of product offerings, varying in price from $80 up to $500 and in some cases more. As a result, a good portion of the customers upgraded to 1 or all of the 3 product offerings, bringing the average initial customer value up from $40 to almost $300 per order.

There are several ways to position and price your upsells.

A good rule of thumb is to have the first upsell equal to or up to 2 times the price as the original product purchased.

Having HUGE gaps in pricing can lead to low results. For example, if your product was $40, it would be more difficult to sell the first upsell for $400. You would have better luck if the price were positioned somewhere close to $40 up to $80.

Now of course the value has to be there in order to justify it.

A good upsell offer can be positioned as a special offer to new customers.

Offer them a 50% savings as a thank you for being a new customer, highlighting the normal price and the price they're paying today.

Test things like video to help boost the results.

Re-targeting:

Have you ever visited a website and found that all of a sudden you're seeing ads for it everywhere?

This isn't the same as the psychological effect where you buy a new car and suddenly you're made aware of that same model everywhere you go.

In this case, the ads are literally following you around. You've been RETARGETED.

A retargeting campaign adds bits of code to your visitors' computers when they come to your site, which signals to online ad networks to display YOUR ads when they visit other sites.

It's an amazingly effective way to increase your visibility and bring people BACK to your site when they don't buy.

Plus, it gives people you already know have some interest in what you offer the impression that you're EVERYWHERE, which boosts your authority and credibility and increases their trust in you.

There are many different ways to go about retargeting in as far as what platform you use to serve your ads.

The great thing about retargeting is you can use it for more than just bringing people back to your site if they haven't purchased.

For example, you can also use it to sell complementary

products to existing customers. The opportunities are literally endless for its uses.

The good part is that we find retargeting campaigns are often a cheaper way to acquire customers.

The reason is because they have seen your site and know about what you offer, so the transition to customer is generally easier.

An example of this working right now is from one of our clients on Facebook ads. We are generating new customers for this client at a rate of $12-$14 per new customer. With the retargeting campaign, we are generating sales conversions at a rate of about $8-$10.

A good use for retargeting to get a prospect back to buy is offering a special bonus or possibly even a discounted price: "Come Back And Save 10% On Our Product."

Your Offer:

Sometimes the best thing you can do for your conversions is to mix up your offer itself.

This may not sound that profound, but if you've already tried optimizing change your offer. Repurpose your product for a different market. If you're selling a premium product, create a low-end version. If you're selling a low-end product, create a premium version.

Here is a case study I heard that is a perfect example of premium vs. low-end:

A prominent manufacturing company of bread machines was

selling its machine in the middle- to low-end of the market but sales dipped. To rectify the situation the company decided to come out with a premium version of the bread machine—one with more bells and whistles than the lower-end model.

The company knew that the majority of those people looking in the market wouldn't buy a machine that was more than double the price. The reason for releasing the premium version was to make the lower-end model more appealing. The result was the sales of the lower-end machine went up over 40%.

When we look at a new campaign, one of the first things we look at is how the product/service is positioned in the market. How is it selling, what is it promising, and so on.

Usually, when an offer is failing or not performing the way it is intended, the reason is because the value proposition isn't high enough. Usually, we can simply add a bonus or re-purpose the value add of the product and see an increase in conversions.

So if you have an offer that isn't quite where it needs to be, take a look at how the value is perceived and see where you can increase the value from there. If your product could sell for $300, it has to be perceived as if customers would be getting a bargain at that particular price point. Then, when customers see the actual price you are charging for it, the offer becomes a no-brainer.

An example of this is in the fitness market, selling home training programs. There are other products selling in the market for $200-$300. Our client is by far the cheapest in the market but the perceived value and everything that is included in the program is positioned at the $200-$300 range. As a result, the programs fly off the shelves.

Sometimes, no matter what you do, the traffic channels don't convert, so you need to look really hard at your offer.

We have had a couple of particular cases where changing the offer made a HUGE difference in the conversions.

The first one was in the beauty products market where the company sends products out monthly with a subscription. When we first started, the company was getting results. but the CPA costs were upwards of $80.

We switched the offer up to give the customers the first shipment for free, and the result was the CPA cost dropped from $80 to less than $10, and the company started to show some serious growth.

Another example was with a company that shipped confectioner sweets and chocolates out on a monthly subscription.

The company had been getting some results, with CPA costs in the mid $20's.

We switched up the offer with a specific landing page to get "double" on their first shipment. As a result, the CPA cost dropped about $10, and the company has seen close to double its active subscription rate in less than 2 months.

Traffic Sources:

Some offers will convert incredibly well with one source of traffic and totally tank with another.

While blaming the traffic for not converting is kind of like golfers blaming their clubs for a bad game, you do sometimes need to try different traffic sources to see what happens.

Really think about where your prospects are and how you can reach them. If you're targeting busy executives, then Facebook advertising probably won't do that well for you.

If you're going after a younger crowd, then buying traffic from Forbes is probably a waste of money.

Things to test: rent lists, buy solo ads, JVs and affiliates, PPC, AdWords, Facebook, LinkedIn, and YouTube.

One other thing to look out for here is not only the source of your traffic but also what landing page you are sending visitors to. Each network has different requirements, such as putting a basic email landing page out on a content network isn't going to work. You would need to cater the message to the medium you are advertising.

Each source should have its own landing page. What converts on Facebook traffic won't necessarily work on Google, and what works on Google most likely won't work on solo ad placements.

Cater your message from ad to landing page for each of the sources of traffic and test them until you find the proper message market match. Targeting of the ads is going to be crucial here as well. You don't want to whittle your targeting down to the point that you can't scale it.

TEN

Attracting Eyeballs

"A good teacher, like a good entertainer first must hold his audience's attention, then he can teach his lesson."
~ John Henrik Clarke

Without a big targeted audience it is tough to gain attraction in any market. It is important that you attract eyeballs—the right eyeballs—to see your solution.

As mentioned earlier, traffic is usually not the problem; there are plenty of places to get traffic.

But often, especially with larger companies, we find that they are bleeding advertising dollars, spending on areas that aren't producing results.

Keeping control gets harder and harder as you expand traffic sources, number of keywords, and number of overall campaigns. So it is easy to see that losing touch with what is working best can become a problem.

In conversion optimization it all starts with the click to the site, and a great place to start optimizing or continue the optimization process is to start with the ad campaigns themselves.

Sometimes, it can be as simple as cutting some losing elements to bring the profitability up dramatically. After all, turning the focus of advertising dollars to the areas producing the best results will not only produce more results but it will also result in increased profitability.

Think of an advertising campaign as a shooting range. You have the target setup at 50 yards and have a shotgun. You fire, and sure, you are going to hit the target with a percentage of the shell fired, but most are going to miss the mark completely.

Now imagine you have a rifle. You fire and hit the bullseye, or at least close to it.

You don't miss the mark or at least you don't miss it by very much. The same thing goes for your ad campaigns. You have to be like the rifle, firing with precision to find the ideal customers—your target.

Narrowing your focus too far can have some limiting factors as well, such as scalability. You can narrow so far that you pick all the customers and are unable to get scalable lasting results from it.

Another way to optimize the ads is to simply work on that,

meaning the ads themselves. Changing the messaging to be more in line with what is being searched or the benefits your product or service provides can lead to more clicks and more eyes on your offer.

Be compelling with your ads. State benefits about why visitors should click, or why they searched for you in the first place.

Making sure you are congruent in the message from the ad to the landing page is one place some people miss the mark as well. Make sure your ad is congruent with what the landing page says.

An example I saw recently was a company advertising an embroidery/screen-printing service on Facebook. The company's ad was good. It said something to the effect of "Get 50% Off Your First Order." But the problem was apparent when you clicked on the ad.

On the landing page there was no mention of the 50% savings or how to redeem the advertised savings. Instead, you were met with a page that said "Get 30% off your order of 6 shirts or more."

There was a BIG congruency issue here and I am guessing the company was having some serious conversion issues and wasting a ton of advertising dollars.

A quick fix would be to put up a basic landing page that stated what the ad said, how to redeem the offer, and a clear call-to-action to "start shopping."

ELEVEN

The Magic Of
Compounding Conversions

"Big doors swing on small hinges."
~ W. Clement Stone

One thing to keep in mind is that in optimization we aren't swinging for the fence every time with the hope of hitting a home run; what we are looking for is continuous slight improvement that will lead to an overall bigger picture win.

Often, people test one element and don't look at the entire picture, which can lead them down a path of actually lowering conversions.

Let's take a look at an example.

Say you are selling a product for $49 and you have an upsell that is $200. You decide to test pricing on your front-end offer and find that $29 converts much higher, but you also find that fewer people also buy your $200 offer. You get more customers but you make less money.

That is why you need to look at your entire sales process as a whole, with customer value and earnings per click at the forefront of your mind at all times.

We are looking for base hits that will lead to an overall improved campaign. Let's take a look at an example of the power this can have for you.

So let's say you have 3 pages in your funnel.

1. A Squeeze Page (which captures visitors' email addresses),

2. A Sales Page (which convinces visitors to add your product to their shopping cart),

3. And A Checkout Page (where visitors enter their credit card information and confirm their purchase)

You don't NEED to have a multi-page funnel to get compound boosts; you can also get them through testing several elements on one page (like button color, call-to-action, pricing options, etc.).

But for the sake of this demonstration, let's look at a simple 3-page funnel so I can show you how Compound Conversion Boosts work.

Now let's plug in some numbers to see how this all works out.

So let's say you have 10,000 visitors a month and your product is $69.95.

Again, you might have more or less traffic and be selling something for a higher or lower price—it doesn't matter; the principle is the same.

Now WITHOUT increasing your traffic and without changing your price, we're going to see what can happen with a few tiny conversion boosts.

You have your opt-in rate, which, again, is the % of visitors who give their email address or other information you are requesting on the Squeeze Page.

You have your click-through rate, which is the percentage of people who hit "add to cart" on your sales page.

And you have your "completed sales," which is the percentage of people who stay on your checkout page and complete their purchase.

So let's start with a 50% opt-in rate, a 4% click-through from the sales page, and a 25% "completed sale" rate. At that price with that much traffic, you're looking at a total revenue of $3497.50.

And those numbers are pretty reasonable.

Now let's see what happens when we get an opt-in rate bump

from 50% to 70%, which, again, is not at all unreasonable. We'll keep the click-through rate the same at 4% and the "completed sale" rate the same at 25%. With that one boost, you've gone from $3497.50 to $4896.50 in total revenue—not bad.

Now let's say you split-test the sales page and you get a small bump from a 4% to a 5% conversion rate.

You still have your 70% opt-in rate and we'll keep the checkout page's conversion rate at 25%. Now your total revenue is $6120.62—again, not bad for a small boost on one page.

Finally, let's say you split-tested your checkout page and saw a bump from a 25% to a 30% conversion rate.

When you compound all the gains you've gotten, you're not looking at a total of $8079.22 in sales.

So as you can see, each small improvement built upon the last, and they compounded for a total boost of **230%** and these are just from small changes.

It's not unusual to sometimes get a 200% or 300% or even 400% conversion boost from a single split-test. It doesn't happen every time, but it does happen.

So from 3 little boosts, you more than doubled your income.

And in a minute I'm going to show you ANOTHER simple strategy that can easily double it again.

This of course is just an example to keep it simple. Often, it looks a bit different than that, but we wanted to keep it simple for the sake of demonstration.

There are some cases where an increase in conversion on the

lead generation squeeze page can actually hurt your sales conversions, putting you in a quality over quantity scenario. But we know our numbers so it doesn't really matter as long as revenue is good on the whole.

With the basic example above, you're probably wondering what kinds of things you can split-test.

We covered a few things in the checklist chapter, but here are a few "small hinges" you can look to test: headline, pricing options, long copy vs short copy, buy button text, video or no video, hybrid pages, call-to-action, offer, product description, page background image, logo vs no logo, menu items, no menu at all, buy button size, colors, images, etc.

Every funnel is different but often, the same things can bring big results no matter what is being sold.

> *A pro tip: You never know what will boost your conversions until you test. You can assume all day long, but assumptions can often be a revenue killer.*

A few years ago we did some work for a large sports training company. On the company's sales video, we tested 3 different versions: a male voice over actor, a female voice over actor, and a more real sounding video with umms and ahhs included.

The marketing director for the company actually wanted the "real sounding" one redone as the other 2 were really good, but for the sake of experiment we agreed to run it as is.

As a result, the real sounding video had almost double the amount of conversions as the second closest video, which was the male voice over actor.

If we would have assumed the voiceover videos would have done better, we would have ultimately missed out on hundreds of thousands in sales revenue.

So never assume anything and test everything.

Increasing Customer Value:

Ok let's continue on our path of the compounding conversion magic, and that is increasing our average customer value.

It is ten times harder and more expensive to get a new customer than it is to get an existing customer to buy more stuff from you.

One of the best ways to get more out of your marketing efforts is to simply get existing customers to buy more stuff from you.

There are hundreds of ways to do this, from upsells during the checkout process, drip email campaigns, affiliate promotions, direct mail campaigns, and even leveraging a call center to sell complementary products.

One of the coolest techniques we have ever seen to get more people back to buy more stuff is something we learned in our work in the supplement industry.

When customers finish with the buying process, immediately give them a credit, which expires, in their account on future purchases.

> *Congratulations Mary,*
> *As a thank you for being a*
> *valued customer we want to give you a*
> *special gift in the form of a $30 gift*
> *certificate on a future order. The $30*
> *credit can be used on any additional*
> *products you want to purchase. This*
> *special credit is only valid until X*
> *date.*
> *To redeem your credit go to*
> *www.mysite.com/gift.*
> *Your credit will automatically be*
> *applied to your order upon checkout.*

This is an extremely powerful value add. Everyone loves free stuff and the sense of urgency with the expiration helps.

If for some reason you aren't able to immediately deposit a credit in an account for that particular customer, a simpler but slightly less effective way is to use coupon codes.

There are hundreds of ways to do this, from upsells during the checkout process, drip email campaigns, affiliate promotions, direct mail campaigns, and even leveraging a call center to sell complementary products.

Other ways to increase customer value include adding and optimizing upsells, increasing back-end product line, selling other people's products as an affiliate, adding a high-ticket program or service, adding a membership or subscription program, or possibly even offering a payment plan.

Again, we know how much a new customer is worth to us from previous chapters. Now it is time to increase that average customer value by continuing with our example.

When we talk about an upsell, this is something you offer to your customers the moment after they've bought something during the checkout process. Thanks to most shopping cart technologies, this is a pretty common practice and they make it quite easy.

The hardest thing to do is to get a visitor to spend that FIRST DOLLAR with you, but once they've crossed that line from prospect to customer, the likelihood that they'll spend even MORE money with you goes up dramatically. Of course if you deliver value.

In fact, a lot of businesses will take a LOSS on their front-end because they make so much money from their upsells and back-end products, as in the example of the SaaS company a couple chapters back.

It's not uncommon for an upsell to go for 4 or 5 times what the "main" front-end product does as far as price but that is what you have to determine.

Let's take our last example and add a single upsell.

Our previous total was $8079.22.

If we add a single upsell at $199.95, and 30% of people end up taking the upsell (which is not at all unusual), you're adding another **$6928.27 to your bottom line.**

That's a 62% increase on your already increased sales numbers.

If you compare the totals (conversion optimization plus a single upsell), we went from $10,000 to $47,910 with the same traffic.

That equals a 379% increase in revenue. Would a 379% increase in sales help your business?

Increase subscription take rate:

We have touted paying close attention to the little things in your marketing on several occasions. Today we bring you another case study that was not only simple but was overlooked as an option.

Before I get into what was done and the results, I first need to set the stage.

The company sells physically shipped goods through a direct-response style sales funnel.

On the company's checkout page, it has 3 options: basically, buy 1, 2, or 4 of this particular product and get additional savings per unit.

The product the company sells is consumable so it will run out, requiring the customer to buy more.

Each of the 3 options comes with a choice to be enrolled in an auto-bill/auto-ship program—you know that fun and amazing recurring continuity program that we all love.

The continuity program was sold as a 10% savings club; buy it today and when we bill you later and ship you the product on the refill, you will save 10%.

On average, 35% of customer chose the recurring subscription with the savings attached to the recurring months' orders.

Customer value was good and so were the re-bill rates.

Now here is where the magic comes in. You are going to be shocked at how simple and obvious this seems but wait until you see the results.

On the subscription that was sold as 10% savings club, instead of paying full-price today and saving on additional billing, we tested it by applying the 10% savings on the checkout page, so customers save 10% on day 1 by joining the subscription program.

Now I told you this was going to be obvious. You might be thinking, "Of course offering 10% would increase the conversion rate."

The magic comes from by HOW MUCH it actually increased.

Before applying the 10% savings on day 1, we mentioned that the take rate for the continuity was 35% on average.

After the test and applying the 10% on day 1, the subscription take rate JUMPED to a whopping 66% of all customers who took the additional savings and joined the subscription program.

Obviously the initial customer value would decrease from the savings, but it more than makes up for it with the continuity re-bills.

Note: The advertised price was based on a 4-unit purchase and the 10% savings were based on that advertised price.

Side bar testing idea: To help increase the customer value on day 1, we are going to test the subscription price as being the same as the advertised price. If customers choose not to join the subscription program, the price will of course be 10% higher.

Remember, our goal to increase conversions is to reduce friction points for the potential customer. In this case, with the increase in conversion rate on the subscriptions, we need to turn our focus to keeping these customers happy, making sure orders go out on time, and figuring out how to get MORE people into the funnel.

We hope this sparks a few ideas to look at in your marketing. We have done plenty of extra options on checkout pages and they seem to work pretty well.

See what you can come up with for on-page checkout options coupled with some additional savings.

TWELVE

The Myth Of Free

"It's much easier to double your business by doubling your conversion rate than by doubling your traffic." ~Jeff Eisenberg

There is no such thing as "free" traffic. It is going to cost you in one way or another, usually in time or money, often both.

Whether it is SEO or affiliate traffic, it doesn't matter.

Now we know that the SEO folks are going to jump all over my case for that statement, but before they do, let's clear the air.

I didn't say that SEO was BAD; we simply said it actually isn't free. We feel that organic traffic is good quality traffic and another method in driving traffic that is highly powerful.

But if your only source is organic and you are just getting

started, know that it will take time to build up enough to be able to actually optimize quickly and effectively.

We have heard some horror stories. In particular, there was a large training organization that had millions of unique visitors coming to its site each month, and literally overnight the company's traffic dropped by two-thirds—talk about a gut check.

Often, we say that organic traffic is not reliable or predictable. You simply can't control it as much as you can paid forms of advertising, at least from a conversion optimization standpoint.

But don't get us a wrong—there is definitely a time and a place for it.

With that said, our preferred method, and where the rocket fuel is added, typically is from paid traffic.

A story that was told by the direct response master, Frank Kern, with regard to paid traffic went something like this:

He said he was in a room with a bunch of successful business owners—people who were doing 7, 8, 9 figures in revenue. He found that those businesses that were driven on organic traffic alone were almost 2 times smaller than those who paid for traffic.

On our basic equation of what it takes for a successful campaign we have talked a lot about the conversion side of the coin and some on the traffic, but now it is time to discuss a little bit more on the traffic side, paid forms in particular.

The secret to mastering paid traffic? The answer is, don't!

Unless you want to focus full-time on becoming a traffic expert, you're better off leaving traffic to the experts and focusing on increasing conversions, customer value and how to branch out.

Why? Because what "works" in traffic is constantly changing. You could spend thousands of dollars learning about traffic, and by the time you were done, most of what you learned would be obsolete.

If you are part of a larger organization that has a traffic team, then you are covered.

But in other instances we recommend having someone who can set it up and handle it for you. We do it all the time for clients, and in other cases, we recommend those that are better at it than us and we stick to optimizing that traffic, working hand-in-hand with the team or agency.

Instead, you're better off focusing on SYSTEMS, CONVERSION, and CUSTOMER VALUE and finding and hiring an expert media buyer to take care of paid traffic for you. Since you already know your EPC, you just need to tell them the maximum CPC you're willing to pay and let them do their thing.

The big secret to success with paid media is an irresistible offer, which we covered earlier on in the book.

Make your media buyer's job easy by giving him or her incredible "ammo" to advertise with.

Here's an example we ran for a client on Facebook that resulted in instant traffic: It was a monthly subscription service that mails you a "box of stuff" each month.

The offer was "sign up for the 'box of stuff' and get your first box free"

Only 200 could claim it on Facebook but 250 people redeemed the coupon code, which equaled customer sharing. TONS of companies do this with dollar trials or free trials on subscriptions. WHY? Because it works! But you've got to have the funnel and the lifetime customer value to back it up!

It's traffic that YOU control, that you can turn up or down depending on your needs.

Paid Traffic lets you scale, and as long as you're tracking your EPC and CPC, you just focus on those sources of traffic that give you a positive ROI.

If you have a good command of PAID TRAFFIC (and you have the other stuff in place), you're in TOTAL CONTROL of your business.

Conclusion

_____

"You don't have to get it perfect, you just have to get it going. Babies don't walk the first time they try, but they eventually get it right." ~ Jack Canfield

It is my sincere hope that you enjoyed this book as much as I enjoyed writing it. With reading the ideas and concepts contained within the preceding pages I hope you now understand the importance of conversion rate optimization.

Due to the importance we have been blessed to have a business devoted to improving the results through this practice. Constant improvement is the name of the game.

As the quote above states, you don't have to get it perfect you just have to get it going. Each day you go without running a test or trying to improve is one day you can't get back and is revenue that you left on the table.

Through testing you can continually stay on the cutting edge in your market, continually understand more about your visitors, and ultimately win the game of marketing.

Test and improve often. Learn from your mistakes and steer the ship accordingly to give your website visitors more of what they want. Solve their problems better than anyone out there and watch your results soar.

Now get out there and start TESTING!

About the authors

Justin Christianson is a self-proclaimed numbers junky. Starting in the Internet marketing game back in 2002, he has a unique ability to find holes in marketing plans and quickly plug them for better ROI.

After several online successes and a successful private consulting practice, Justin, along with Manish Punjabi, co-founded Conversion Fanatics, a full service conversion rate optimization company that serves mid- to large-scale clients increase the effectiveness of their online marketing campaigns and website conversions.

Justin loves the outdoors, whether it is playing golf, swimming with his kids, or boating out on the lake. He is an avid reader, striving each day to hone his skills in marketing, business, and life.

Manish Punjabi lives in a world where anything is possible. He's a 8 year practitioner of using conversion optimization, strategic positioning, and media buying to help companies grow exponentially. His ideas have helped both startups and large organizations cut waste while building scalable campaigns and sales funnels. He holds a BA in Economics and Psychology from the University of Texas.

About Conversion Fanatics

Defenders of all things awesome in digital marketing and conversion optimization.

We possess special online marketing powers. Our Mission: To be better than we were yesterday and save online advertisers from un-profitable campaigns.

In 2013 co-founders, Manish Punjabi and Justin Christianson, after individually selling their multiple 7 figure online publishing businesses, heard the calls of distress from online advertisers and they took action.

Conversion Fanatics was born and is made up of some of the smartest minds in marketing with the goal to save failing campaigns one test at a time.

Since then they have worked on hundreds of campaigns and have ran thousands of tests in multiple industries leaving a wake of staggering results improvement.

We continue to use our powers for good by creating proprietary marketing practices, client consulting and blog content. We ward off evil-doers and helps business owners achieve and exceed their wildest marketing and conversion goals.

Headquartered out of wonderful Austin TX, we make the most of our in-the-trenches experience and today's cutting edge marketing strategies to help innocent businesses defend themselves against ineffective marketing campaigns and achieve better visitor engagement and results.

"Our goal of founding Conversion Fanatics, is to provide valuable advice and provide the bandwidth to effectively implement best practices and data driven optimization and marketing strategies to make a difference in your business, today, not weeks and months. Our passion and drive is to be the #1 resource for online advertisers!"

If you are struggling with your marketing efforts or simple "want more" then I encourage you to reach out to us for a no obligation "conversion acceleration session".

www.ConversionFanatics.com

Acknowledgments

Thank You!

Special thanks to my wife Jodi for being by my side and supporting me through it all.

To my family and friends who have always believed in me.

To my awesome business partner, Manish, who had a BIG hand in getting this book out there through his contribution and the results he helps us get for our clients.

A sincere thank you to Mike Dillard for being my first mentor, for seeing something in me that others didn't, and giving me a chance to grow as a businessperson and marketer early on.

To Michaela for tearing this book apart and making my

ramblings something people can actually read.

To Rob for the AMAZING cover art, thanks!

To our team at Conversion Fanatics, we simply couldn't do it without you. Your drive and determination is what makes us great.

To all our amazing clients, you push us to be better and continue to think outside the box. It is a pleasure helping you grow your companies.

Thanks to all the marketers and business people who have taught me so much in my years of being in the trenches.

To name a few... Eric Graham for paving the way for CRO. Matt Gill for being such a great friend, amazingly smart marketer, and someone who I have looked up to for years. Ryan Levesque for not only the foreword but doing what you do by getting to know website visitors to better deliver products and services. Justin Tupper for being a long time friend, mentor, and inspiration to go after bigger and better. All the authors who have come before me and shared their knowledge, I appreciate you. There are many many more that I would like to personally thank which I simply can't do or this book would be dozens of pages longer.

Finally a big thanks to YOU for picking up this book and wanting more out of your advertising. THANKS!

Connect With The Author

Facebook: Facebook.com/conversionfanatics

Twitter: @convfanatics

LinkedIn: conversionfanatics.com/linkedin

Email: support@conversionfanatics.com

Website: www.ConversionFanatics.com